READY NOTES

to accompany

MANAGERIAL ACCOUNTING
CONCEPTS FOR PLANNING, CONTROL, DECISION MAKING

Seventh Edition

Ray H. Garrison
Brigham Young University
Eric W. Noreen
University of Washington

IRWIN
Burr Ridge, Illinois
Boston, Massachusetts
Sydney, Australia

Printed in the United States of America.

ISBN 0-256-14978-X

2 3 4 5 6 7 8 9 0 WCB 0 9 8 7 6 5 4 3

Table of Contents

THE PLANNING AND CONTROL CYCLE

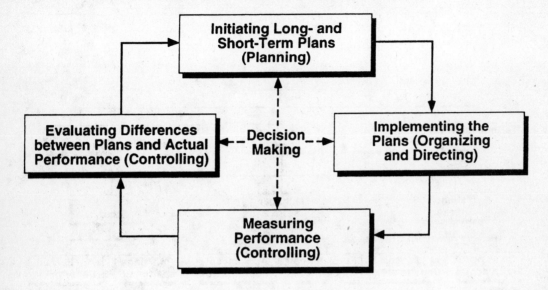

AN ORGANIZATION CHART

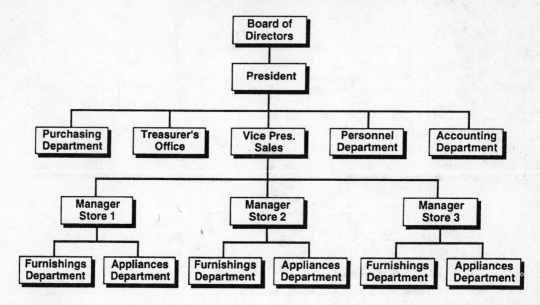

STANDARDS OF ETHICAL CONDUCT
FOR MANAGEMENT ACCOUNTANTS
(adapted from IMA)

COMPETENCE
- Maintain professional competence.
- Follow laws, regulations, and standards.
- Prepare complete and clear reports and recommendations after appropriate analysis.

CONFIDENTIALITY
- Don't disclose confidential information.
- Ensure that subordinates do not disclose confidential information.
- Do not use confidential information for personal gain or advantage.

INTEGRITY
- Avoid actual or apparent conflicts of interest.
- Refuse gifts, favors, or hospitality that might influence objectivity.
- Refrain from subverting the organization's legitimate objectives.
- Recognize and communicate personal limitations.
- Communicate unfavorable as well as favorable information and opinions.
- Refrain from actions that discredit the profession.

OBJECTIVITY
- Communicate information fairly and objectively.
- Fully disclose all information that could be expected to influence a user's understanding.

A SUMMARY OF COST TERMS

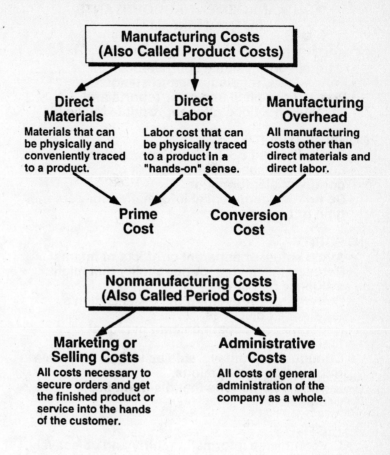

**Manufacturing Costs
(Also Called Product Costs)**

Direct Materials
Materials that can be physically and conveniently traced to a product.

Direct Labor
Labor cost that can be physically traced to a product in a "hands-on" sense.

Manufacturing Overhead
All manufacturing costs other than direct materials and direct labor.

Prime Cost

Conversion Cost

**Nonmanufacturing Costs
(Also Called Period Costs)**

Marketing or Selling Costs
All costs necessary to secure orders and get the finished product or service into the hands of the customer.

Administrative Costs
All costs of general administration of the company as a whole.

COST OF GOODS MANUFACTURED

Rider Company
Schedule of Cost of Goods Manufactured

Direct materials:
Beginning raw materials inventory . . . $ 10,000
Add: Purchases of raw materials 200,000
Raw materials available for use 210,000
Deduct: Ending raw materials inventory . 30,000
Raw materials used in production $180,000
Direct labor 270,000
Manufacturing overhead:
Indirect materials 5,000
Indirect labor 100,000
Utilities, factory 80,000
Property taxes, factory 36,000
Insurance, factory 9,000
Equipment rental 70,000
Depreciation, factory 120,000
Total overhead costs 420,000
Total manufacturing costs 870,000
Add: Beginning work in process inventory . 40,000
910,000
Deduct: Ending work in process inventory . 60,000
Cost of goods manufactured $850,000

* *

Cost of goods sold:
Beginning finished goods inventory $130,000
Add: Cost of goods manufactured 850,000
Goods available for sale 980,000
Deduct: Ending finished goods inventory 80,000
Cost of goods sold $900,000

COST FLOWS IN A MANUFACTURING FIRM
(Exhibit 2-5)

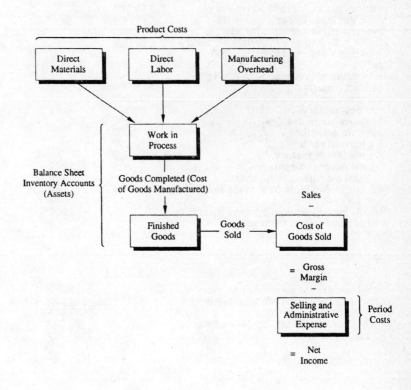

COST BEHAVIOR

In terms of behavior, costs are frequently divided into two categories—<u>variable</u> and <u>fixed</u>.

VARIABLE COSTS

Variable cost behavior can be summarized as follows:

Variable Cost Behavior	
In Total	*Per Unit*
Total variable cost increases and decreases in proportion to changes in activity.	**Variable costs remain constant per unit.**

EXAMPLE: A company manufactures microwave ovens. Each oven requires a timing device that costs $30. The per unit and total cost of the timing device at various levels of activity would be:

Cost per Timing Device	Number of Ovens Produced	Total Variable Cost—Timing Devices
$30	1	$ 30
30	10	300
30	100	3,000
30	200	6,000

FIXED COSTS

Fixed cost behavior can be summarized as follows:

Fixed Cost Behavior

In Total	Per Unit
Total fixed cost is not affected by changes in activity (i.e., total fixed cost remains constant even if activity changes).	Fixed costs decrease per unit as the activity level rises and increase per unit as the activity level falls.

EXAMPLE: Assume again that a company manufactures microwave ovens. The company pays $9,000 per month to rent its factory building. The total and per unit cost of the rent at various levels of activity would be:

Rent Cost per Month	Number of Ovens Produced	Rent Cost per Timing Device
$9,000	1	$9,000
9,000	10	900
9,000	100	90
9,000	200	45

OTHER COST TERMS

DIRECT AND INDIRECT COSTS

A <u>direct cost</u> is a cost that can be obviously and physically traced to the particular segment under consideration. For example, if the segment under consideration is a product line, then the materials and labor involved in the manufacture of the product line would both be direct costs.

An <u>indirect cost</u> is a cost that must be allocated in order to be assigned to the segment under consideration. Manufacturing overhead, for example, would be an indirect cost of a product line.

i.e. personnel dept, Facilities mgmt., etc

CONTROLLABLE COSTS

A cost is considered to be <u>controllable</u> at a particular level of the organization if managers at that level have the power to authorize the cost.

There is a time dimension to controllability. Costs that are controllable over the long run may not be controllable over the short run.

DIFFERENTIAL COST

Any cost that is present under one alternative but is absent in whole or in part under another alternative is known as a <u>differential cost</u>.

EXAMPLE: Bill is employed as a lifeguard. He has been offered a job in an auto service center. The differential revenue and costs between the two jobs are:

	Life-guard	Auto service center	Differential costs and revenues
Monthly salary	$900	$1,200	$300
Monthly expenses:			
Commuting	30	90	60
Uniform rental	—	50	50
Union dues	10	—	(10)
Total monthly expenses . .	40	140	100
Net monthly income	$860	$1,060	$200

OPPORTUNITY COST

An <u>opportunity cost</u> is the potential benefit that is lost or sacrificed when selecting one course of action makes it necessary to give up an alternative course of action.

EXAMPLE: Linda is employed in the campus bookstore and is paid $20 per day. One of her roommates is getting married and Linda would like to attend the wedding, but she would have to miss a day of work. If she attends the wedding, the $20 in lost wages will be an opportunity cost of attending the wedding.

EXAMPLE: Fred is employed as a computer programmer with a company that pays him $21,000 per year. He is thinking about leaving the company in order to return to school to get an MBA degree. If Fred returns to school, the $21,000 in lost salary will be an opportunity cost of seeking further education.

SUNK COST

A <u>sunk cost</u> is a cost that has already been incurred and that cannot be changed by any decision made now or in the future.

ACCOUNTING FOR LABOR COSTS

Labor costs can be categorized as follows:

Direct labor	Indirect labor (part of manufacturing overhead)	Other labor costs
(Discussed earlier)	Janitors Supervisors Materials handlers Engineers Night security guards Maintenance workers	Idle time Overtime premium Labor fringe benefits

IDLE TIME

Idle time represents the cost of direct labor workers who are unable to perform their assignments due to machine breakdowns, material shortages, power failures, and the like. The cost of idle time is often added to manufacturing overhead.

EXAMPLE: An assembly line worker is idle for 2 hours during the week due to a power failure. If the worker is paid $10 per hour and works a normal 40 hour week, labor cost would be allocated as follows between direct labor and manufacturing overhead:

Direct labor cost ($10 X 38 hours) $380
Manufacturing overhead cost ($10 x 2 hours)   20
   Total cost for the week $400

OVERTIME PREMIUM

The overtime premium paid to all factory workers (direct labor as well as indirect labor) is considered to be part of manufacturing overhead.

EXAMPLE: Assume again that an assembly line worker is paid $10 per hour. The worker is paid time and a half for overtime (time in excess of 40 hours per week). During a given week this employee works 46 hours and has no idle time. Labor cost would be allocated as follows:

Direct labor cost ($10 X 46 hours)	$460
Manufacturing overhead cost ($5 X 6 hours) . . .	30
Total cost for the week	$490

LABOR FRINGE BENEFITS

Labor fringe benefits are made up of employment related costs paid by the employer. These costs are handled in two different ways:

1. Many firms treat all such costs as indirect labor and add them to manufacturing overhead.

2. Other firms treat that portion of fringe benefits that relates to direct labor as additional direct labor cost.

APPLICATION OF OVERHEAD

It is usually easy to assign materials and labor costs to products and services. Why?

It is difficult, however, to assign overhead costs to products and services. Why?

PREDETERMINED OVERHEAD RATES

A <u>predetermined overhead rate</u> is used to assign overhead cost to products and services. It is:
- Based on estimated data.
- Established before the period begins.

Why Use Estimated Data?

1. Waiting until the year is over to determine actual overhead costs would be too late. Managers need to cost jobs immediately.

2. Overhead rates, if based on actual costs and activity, would vary substantially from month to month. Much of this variation would be due to random changes in activity.

PREDETERMINED OVERHEAD RATE FORMULA

The formula for computing a predetermined overhead rate is:

$$\frac{\text{Estimated total manufacturing overhead costs}}{\text{Estimated total activity (DLH, MH, etc.)}} = \frac{\text{Predetermined}}{\text{Overhead Rate}}$$

EXAMPLE: Assume that Parker Company allocates overhead costs to jobs (and therefore to products) on the basis of machine-hours. For the coming year the company estimates that it will incur $600,000 in manufacturing overhead costs and work 75,000 machine-hours. The company's predetermined overhead rate would be:

$$\frac{\$600,000}{75,000 \text{ MH}} = \$8/\text{MH}$$

APPLICATION OF OVERHEAD TO JOBS

The process of assigning overhead to jobs is known as the application of overhead.

EXAMPLE: Refer to the data for Parker Company above. If a particular job requires $5,000 for direct materials, $3,000 for direct labor, and 500 machine-hours then the computed cost of the job would be:

Direct materials	$ 5,000
Direct labor	3,000
Manufacturing overhead (500 MH x $8/MH)	4,000
Total cost	$12,000

MATERIALS REQUISITION FORM
(Exhibit 3-1)

Materials Requisition Number   14873   Date   March 2, 19x2

Job Number to Be Charged   2B47

Department   Milling

Description	Quantity	Unit Cost	Total Cost
M46 Housing	150	$1.64	$246
G7 Connector	300	1.38	414
			$660

Authorized
Signature   *Bill White*

EMPLOYEE TIME TICKET
(Exhibit 3-3)

Time Ticket No. 843   Date March 3, 19x2

Employee Mary Holden   Station 4

Started	Ended	Time Completed	Rate	Amount	Job Number
7:00	12:00	5.0	$9	$45	2B47
12:30	2:30	2.0	9	18	2B50
2:30	3:30	1.0	9	9	Maintenance
Totals		8.0		$72	

Supervisor _R. W. Pace_

JOB COST SHEET
(Exhibit 3-4)

JOB COST SHEET

Job Number   2B47   Date Initiated   March 2, 19x2
                                          Date Completed   March 8, 19x2

Department   Milling
Item   Special order coupling   Units Completed   150
For Stock

Direct Materials		Direct Labor			Manufacturing Overhead		
Req. No.	Amount	Ticket	Hours	Amount	Hours	Rate	Amount
14873	$ 660	843	5	$ 45	27	$8/DLH	$216
14875	506	846	8	60			
14912	238	850	4	21			
	$1,404	851	10	54			
			27	$180			

Cost Summary		Units Shipped		
Direct Materials	$1,404	Date	Number	Balance
Direct Labor	$ 180	3/8/x2	—	150
Manufacturing Overhead	$ 216			
Total Cost	$1,800			
Unit Cost	$ 12*			

* $1,800 ÷ 150 units = $12 per unit.

THE FLOW OF DOCUMENTS IN A JOB-ORDER COSTING SYSTEM

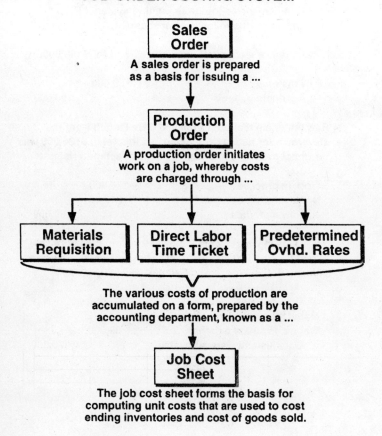

Sales Order

A sales order is prepared as a basis for issuing a ...

Production Order

A production order initiates work on a job, whereby costs are charged through ...

Materials Requisition   **Direct Labor Time Ticket**   **Predetermined Ovhd. Rates**

The various costs of production are accumulated on a form, prepared by the accounting department, known as a ...

Job Cost Sheet

The job cost sheet forms the basis for computing unit costs that are used to cost ending inventories and cost of goods sold.

JOB-ORDER COSTING EXAMPLE

1. Reeder Company has a job-order costing system. Prepare journal entries for the following transactions:

   a. Raw materials were purchased on account for $150,000.

Raw materials	150,000	
Accounts payable		150,000

   b. Raw materials that cost $160,000 were issued from the storeroom for use in production. Of this total, $136,000 was for direct materials and $24,000 for indirect materials.

Work in process	136,000	
Manufacturing overhead	24,000	
Raw materials		160,000

   c. The following costs were incurred for employee services: Direct Labor, $200,000; Indirect Labor, $85,0000; Selling and Administrative Wages and Salaries, $90,000.

Work in process	200,000	
Manufacturing overhead	85,000	
Wage and salary expense	90,000	
Salaries and wages payable		375,000

JOB-ORDER COSTING EXAMPLE (cont'd)

d. Utility costs of $40,000 were incurred in the factory.

    Manufacturing overhead 40,000
       Accounts payable (or cash)   40,000

e. Prepaid insurance in the amount of $20,000 expired during the year. (80% related to factory operations and 20% to selling and administration.)

    Manufacturing overhead 16,000
    Insurance expense 4,000
       Prepaid insurance   20,000

f. Advertising costs of $100,000 were incurred during the year.

    Advertising expense 100,000
       Accounts payable (or cash)   100,000

g. Depreciation of $145,000 was accrued for the year on factory assets and $15,000 on selling and administrative assets.

    Manufacturing overhead 145,000
    Depreciation expense 15,000
       Accumulated depreciation   160,000

JOB-ORDER COSTING EXAMPLE (cont'd)

h. Manufacturing overhead was applied to jobs. The company's predetermined overhead rate was based on the following estimates: Manufacturing overhead, $315,000; Direct labor cost, $210,0000.

$$\frac{\$315,000}{\$210,000} = 1.5 \text{ or } 150\%$$

Since the total direct labor cost incurred was $200,000, the total manufacturing overhead applied to work in process was 150% of this amount or $300,000. The journal entry to record this is:

Work in process	300,000	
Manufacturing overhead		300,000

i. Goods that cost $650,000 to manufacture were completed and transferred to the finished goods warehouse.

Finished goods	650,000	
Work in process		650,000

j. Sales for the year (all on credit) totalled $900,000.

Accounts receivable	900,000	
Sales		900,000

k. The goods that were sold had cost $600,000 to manufacture.

Cost of goods sold	600,000	
Finished goods		600,000

JOB-ORDER COSTING EXAMPLE (cont'd)

2. T-accounts are illustrated below for the various manufacturing accounts (opening balances are assumed).

Raw Materials			
Bal.	20,000		
(a)	150,000	160,000	(b)
Bal.	10,000		

Manufacturing Overhead			
(b)	24,000	300,000	(h)
(c)	85,000		
(d)	40,000		
(e)	16,000		
(g)	145,000		
Bal	10,000		

Work in Process			
Bal.	74,000		
(b)	136,000	650,000	(i)
(c)	200,000		
(h)	300,000		
Bal.	60,000		

Finished Goods			
Bal.	40,000		
(i)	650,000	600,000	(k)
Bal.	90,000		

Cost of Goods Sold	
(k) 600,000	

a) Purchase of raw materials.
b) Issue of materials.
c) Labor costs.
d) Factory utility costs.
e) Factory insurance costs.

g) Depreciation on factory assets.
h) Apply manufacturing overhead.
i) WIP completed.
k) Finished Goods sold.

JOB-ORDER COSTING EXAMPLE (cont'd)

3. Disposition of under- or overapplied overhead.

   a. Close the balance to Cost of Goods Sold:

      Cost of goods sold 10,000
         Manufacturing overhead   10,000

or

   b. Allocate the balance to Work In Process, Finished Goods, and Cost of Goods Sold.

	Ending Balance	Percent of Total
Work in Process	$ 60,000	8%
Finished Goods	90,000	12
Cost of Goods Sold	600,000	80
Total	$750,000	100%

The journal entry to record the allocation would be:

      Work in process (8% of $10,000) . . . 800
      Finished goods (12% of $10,000) . . 1,200
      Cost of goods sold (80% of $10,000) 8,000
         Manufacturing overhead   10,000

JOB-ORDER COSTING EXAMPLE (cont'd)

4. Reeder Company's income statement for the year (assuming that the underapplied overhead is closed directly to Cost of Goods Sold) would be:

Reeder Company
Income Statement

Sales		$900,000
Cost of goods sold ($600,000 + $10,000)		610,000
Gross Margin		290,000
Less selling and administrative expenses:		
Wage and salary expense	$ 90,000	
Insurance expense	4,000	
Advertising expense	100,000	
Depreciation expense	15,000	209,000
Net income		$ 81,000

UNDER- AND OVERAPPLIED OVERHEAD

Since predetermined overhead rates are based on estimated data, at the end of an accounting period overhead costs are normally either <u>underapplied</u> or <u>overapplied</u>. In this example, overhead is underapplied by $10,000 which can be determined by examining the balance in the Manufacturing Overhead account:

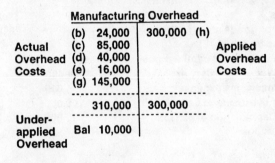

The discrepancy of $10,000 between the actual overhead costs and the applied overhead costs is called underapplied overhead in this case because actual overhead costs that were incurred exceeded the overhead costs that were applied to inventory.

Alternatively, the amount of the under- or overapplied overhead can be determined as follows:

Actual overhead costs incurred	$310,000
Applied overhead costs (150% x $200,000)	300,000
Underapplied overhead	$ 10,000

COST FLOWS IN A JOB-ORDER COSTING SYSTEM
(Exhibit 3-13)

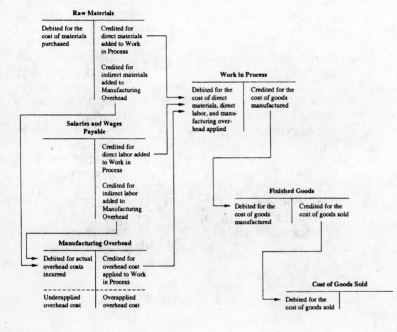

DIFFERENCES BETWEEN JOB-ORDER AND PROCESS COSTING

Job-Order Costing	Process Costing
1. Many different jobs are worked on during each period, with each job having different production requirements.	1. A single product is produced either on a continuous basis or for long periods of time. All units are identical.
2. Costs are accumulated by job.	2. Costs are accumulated by department.
3. The *job cost sheet* is the key document for accumulating costs.	3. The *departmental production report* is the key document showing the accumulation and disposition of costs.
4. Unit costs are computed *by job* on the job cost sheet.	4. Unit costs are computed *by department* on the department production report.

T-ACCOUNT MODEL OF PROCESS COSTING FLOWS
(Exhibit 4-4)

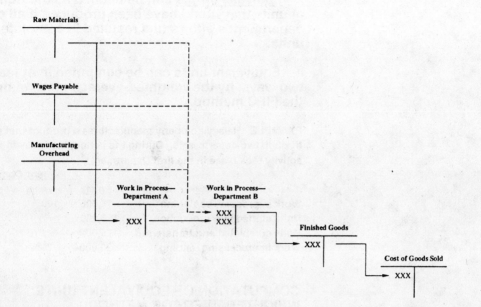

EQUIVALENT UNITS

• <u>Equivalent units</u> can be defined as the number of units that would have been produced if all of a department's efforts had resulted in completed units.

• Equivalent units can be computed in at least two ways: by the weighted-average method or by the FIFO method.

EXAMPLE: Halsey company manufactures a product that goes through two departments. During the period, the following activity took place in the first Department:

		Percent Completed	
	Units	Materials	Conversion
Work in process, beginning	15,000	100%	80%
Units started into production	180,000		
Units completed and transferred	175,000		
Work in processing, ending	20,000	70%	30%

COMPUTATION OF EQUIVALENT UNITS: WEIGHTED-AVERAGE METHOD

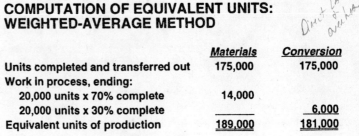

	Materials	Conversion
Units completed and transferred out	175,000	175,000
Work in process, ending:		
20,000 units x 70% complete	14,000	
20,000 units x 30% complete		6,000
Equivalent units of production	189,000	181,000

• The weighted-average method blends costs and units from beginning inventory with costs and units added during the current period. The equivalent units of production under the weighted-average method refers to the equivalent units inherent in both ending inventory and in the units transferred out, regardless of the periods in which the work was done.

COMPUTATION OF EQUIVALENT UNITS: FIFO METHOD

• The FIFO method separates the equivalent units in beginning inventory from the work done during the current period, rather than blending them together as in the weighted-average method. The equivalent units of production under the FIFO method refers only to the work performed during the current period. Under FIFO, it is assumed the beginning inventory is completed before any new units are started.

	Materials	*Conversion*
Work to complete beginning inventory		
15,000 units x (100% — 100%)*	—	
15,000 units x (100% — 80%)*		3,000
Units started and completed this period**	160,000	160,000
Work in process, ending:		
20,000 units x 70% complete	14,000	
20,000 units x 30% complete		6,000
Equivalent units of production	174,000	169,000

* Work required to *complete* the units in beginning inventory.
** 175,000 units - 15,000 units = 160,000 units.

OVERVIEW OF EQUIVALENT UNITS

Weighted-Average Method

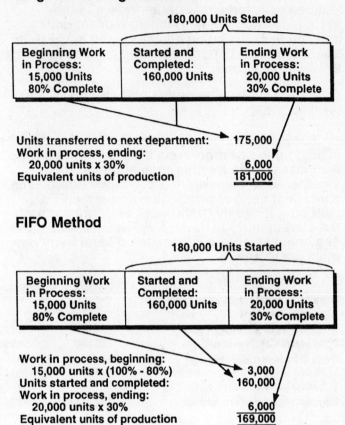

180,000 Units Started

Beginning Work in Process: 15,000 Units 80% Complete	Started and Completed: 160,000 Units	Ending Work in Process: 20,000 Units 30% Complete

Units transferred to next department: 175,000
Work in process, ending:
   20,000 units x 30%   6,000
Equivalent units of production   <u>181,000</u>

FIFO Method

180,000 Units Started

Beginning Work in Process: 15,000 Units 80% Complete	Started and Completed: 160,000 Units	Ending Work in Process: 20,000 Units 30% Complete

Work in process, beginning:
   15,000 units x (100% - 80%)   3,000
Units started and completed: 160,000
Work in process, ending:
   20,000 units x 30%   6,000
Equivalent units of production   <u>169,000</u>

PRODUCTION REPORT

The purpose of the production report is to summarize for the manager all of the activity that takes place in a department's Work In Process account for a period.

There are three separate (though highly interrelated) parts to the production report:

1. A quantity schedule with equivalent units.

2. Computation of unit costs.

3. A reconciliation of all cost flows into and out of the department during the period.

EXAMPLE:

	Units	Materials	Conversion
Work in process, beginning:			
Units in process	10,000		
Stages of completion		100%	90%
Cost of beginning inventory		$3,520	$7,208
Units started into production	190,000		
Costs added by the department during the current period		$74,480	$148,192
Units completed and transferred	180,000		
Work in process, ending:			
Units in process	20,000		
Stage of completion		100%	25%

QUANTITY SCHEDULE AND EQUIVALENT UNITS: WEIGHTED-AVERAGE METHOD

The purpose of the quantity schedule is to account for the physical flow of units through a department for a period.

	Quantity Schedule	Materials	Conversion
Units to be accounted for:			
Units in process, beginning	10,000		
Units started into production	190,000		
Total units to account for	200,000		
Units accounted for as follows:			
Units completed and transferred	180,000	180,000	180,000
Units in process, ending	20,000	20,000	5,000
Total units accounted for	200,000	200,000	185,000

COMPUTATION OF UNIT COSTS: WEIGHTED-AVERAGE METHOD

	Total	Materials	Conversion
Work in process, beginning	$ 10,728	$ 3,520	$ 7,208
Costs added by the department	222,672	74,480	148,192
Total cost (a)	$233,400	$78,000	$155,400
Equivalent units (b)		200,000	185,000
Unit cost (a) ÷ (b)		$0.39	$0.84

COST RECONCILIATION:
WEIGHTED-AVERAGE METHOD

	Total Cost	Equivalent Units	
		Materials	Conversion
Cost accounted for as follows:			
Transferred out			
Materials @ $0.39 per EU	$ 70,200	180,000	
Conversion @ $0.84 per EU	151,200		180,000
Total transferred out	221,400		
Work in process, ending:			
Materials @ $0.39 per EU	7,800	20,000	
Conversion @ $0.84 per EU	4,200		5,000
Total work in process, ending	12,000		
Total cost accounted for	$233,400		

QUANTITY SCHEDULE AND EQUIVALENT UNITS: FIFO

	Quantity Schedule	Equivalent Units Materials	Conversion
Units to be accounted for:			
Units in process, beginning	10,000		
Units started into production	190,000		
Total units to account for	200,000		
Units accounted for as follows:			
Units completed and transferred			
Units from beginning inventory	10,000	—	1,000*
Units started and completed**	170,000	170,000	170,000
Units in process, ending	20,000	20,000	5,000
Total units accounted for	200,000	190,000	176,000

* (100% - 90%) x 10,000
* 180,000 units - 10,000 units = 170,000 units

Note: Unlike the weighted-average method, FIFO equivalent units refer to just the equivalent units for the work performed in the current period.

COMPUTATION OF UNIT COSTS:
FIFO METHOD

	Total	Materials	Conversion
Costs added by the department (a)	222,672	74,480	148,192
Equivalent units (b)		190,000	176,000
Unit cost (a) ÷ (b)		$0.392	$0.842

Note: Unlike the weighted-average method, under the FIFO method only the costs added by the department during the current month are considered in the computation of the unit costs. The costs of beginning inventory are not included in the unit cost computations under the FIFO method.

CONTRAST IN UNIT COSTS:
WEIGHTED-AVERAGE AND FIFO METHODS

Conversion costs provide a good illustration:

	Conversion Costs	
	Equivalent Units	Cost
Work performed in previous periods		
Beginning Inventory	9,000	$ 7,208
Work performed this period		
Completion of beginning inventory	1,000	not applicable
Units started and completed	170,000	not applicable
Ending Inventory	5,000	not applicable
Total	176,000	$148,192

FIFO method

Unit cost of equivalent units in beginning inventory:

$$\frac{\$7,208}{9,000 \text{ units}} = \$0.801 \text{ per unit}$$

Unit cost of equivalent units for work performed this period:

$$\frac{\$148,192}{176,000 \text{ units}} = \$0.842 \text{ per unit}$$

Weighted-average method

Unit cost of *all* equivalent units:

$$\frac{\$7,208 + \$148,192}{9,000 \text{ units} + 176,000 \text{ units}} = \$0.84 \text{ per unit}$$

Note: The weighted-average method averages the two categories of FIFO unit costs using their equivalent units as weights.

$$\frac{\frac{\$7,208}{9,000} \times 9,000 + \frac{\$148,192}{176,000} \times 176,000}{9,000 + 176,000} = \frac{\$7,208 + \$148,192}{9,000 + 176,000}$$

COST RECONCILIATION:
FIFO METHOD

	Total Cost	Equivalent Units Materials	Conversion
Transferred out:			
Units from beginning inventory:			
Cost in beginning inventory	$ 10,728		
Cost to complete these units:			
Materials @ $0.392 per EU		—	
Conversion @ $0.842 per EU	842		1,000
Total	11,570		
Units started and completed:			
Materials @ $0.392 per EU	66,640	170,000	
Conversion @ $0.842 per EU	143,140		170,000
Total	209,780		
Total cost transferred	221,350		
Work in process, ending:			
Materials @ $0.392 per EU	7,840	20,000	
Conversion @ $0.842 per EU	4,210		5,000
Total work in process, ending	12,050		
Total cost accounted for	$233,400		

A COMPARISON OF PRODUCTION REPORTS

Weighted-Average Method FIFO Method

Quantity Schedule and Equivalent Units

Weighted-Average Method	FIFO Method
1. The quantity schedule includes all units transferred out in a single figure.	1. The quantity schedule divides units transferred out into two parts — units in beginning inventory and units started and completed during the current period.
2. In computing equivalent units, units in beginning inventory are treated as if they were started and completed during the current period.	2. Only work needed to *complete* units in the beginning inventory is included in the equivalent units.

Total and Unit Costs

1. The "Cost to be accounted for" part of the report is the same for both methods.

Weighted-Average Method	FIFO Method
2. Costs in beginning inventory are added to current period costs.	2. Only current period costs are included in unit costs.
3. Unit costs contain some cost from the prior period.	3. Unit costs contain only costs from the current period.

Cost Reconciliation

Weighted-Average Method	FIFO Method
1. All units transferred out are treated the same.	1. Units transferred out are divided into two groups: units in beginning inventory and units started during the period.

2. Units in ending inventory have cost applied to them in the same way under both methods.

JUST IN TIME (JIT) INVENTORY SYSTEMS

<u>Just In Time</u> (JIT) means that raw materials are received *just in time* to go into production, parts arrive at work stations *just in time* to be assembled into products, and products are completed *just in time* to be shipped to customers. In a true JIT system there are almost no inventories.

In JIT, parts and material are "pulled" through the assembly process as needed.

- At the final assembly stage, a signal is sent to the preceding workstation as to the exact amount of parts and materials needed over the next few hours for the final assembly of products.

- A similar signal is sent back through each preceding workstation. Thus, all workstations respond to the "pull" exerted by the final assembly stage.

The "pull" approach is in contrast to the "push" approach used in conventional production control systems. In a push system, work in process is pushed through the factory from one workstation to the next with little regard to when it is actually needed. In a push system, the overriding concern is often to keep all the workstations busy.

KEY ELEMENTS IN A JIT SYSTEM

Five key elements are involved in a successful JIT system:

1. *Develop long-term relationships with a few high quality suppliers who commit to making frequent deliveries in small lots.*

2. *Improve the plant layout to reduce the distances work in process must travel.* Traditionally, all drill presses are put in one location, all milling machines in another, and so on. Instead, under JIT all of the different machines required to make a major component are grouped together in a "cell."

3. *Reduce setup time.* This increases the speed with which a company can respond to customer orders and reduces the need for inventories.

4. *Implement a Total Quality Control (TQC) program to reduce defect rates.* When defect rates are high, excess work in process is needed to ensure that there are enough defect-free finished goods at the end of the process to meet customer orders.

5. *Develop a flexible work force.* Cells contain many different machines that each individual should know how to run. In addition, workers are their own quality inspectors and perform much of their own maintenance.

BENEFITS OF A JIT SYSTEM

The following are often cited as major benefits of a JIT system:

1. Worker productivity is improved due to improved plant layout.

2. Setup time is reduced, resulting in smaller batch sizes.

3. Total production time is decreased, resulting in greater output and quicker response to customer needs.

4. Through TQC, defects are reduced.

5. Inventories are reduced.

6. Working capital is bolstered by releasing funds previously tied up in inventories.

7. Space is made available for more productive uses.

JIT AND MANUFACTURING TIME

Much of what is done in JIT is aimed at reducing manufacturing time which can be expressed as the sum of four elements:

> Processing time
> + Inspection time
> + Move time
> + <u>Wait time</u>
> <u>Manufacturing time</u>

Only processing time adds value to the product. Inspection time, move time, and wait time are all non-value added activities and should be eliminated to the extent possible.

JIT reduces non-value added time:

- Decreasing set-up time reduces wait time.

- Improving plant layout reduces move time.

- Eliminating defects reduces inspection time.

ACTIVITY-BASED COSTING

An activity is any event or transaction that is a cost driver. Examples of activities that are cost drivers include:

- Machine setups.
- Purchase orders.
- Quality inspections.
- Production orders.
- Blood tests run.

- Maintenance requests.
- Machine time.
- Power consumed.
- Beds occupied.
- Flight-hours logged.

Activity-based costing improves costing systems in three ways:

1. *It increases the number of cost pools used to accumulate overhead costs.* Rather than accumulate all overhead costs in a single, companywide pool (or in departments), costs are accumulated by activity.

2. *It changes the bases used to assign overhead cost to products.* Rather than assigning costs on the basis of a measure of volume (such as direct labor-hours or machine-hours), costs are assigned on the basis of the activities that generate the costs.

3. *It changes the nature of many overhead costs.* Costs that were formerly indirect (depreciation, power, inspection) are traced to specific activities.

ACTIVITY-BASED COSTING EXAMPLE

Sarver Company manufactures 4,000 units of Product A and 20,000 units of Product B each year. The company currently uses direct labor-hours to assign overhead cost to products. The predetermined overhead rate is:

$$\frac{\text{Manufacturing overhead cost}}{\text{Direct labor-hours}} = \frac{\$900,000}{50,000} = \$18/\text{DLH}$$

Product A requires 2.5 DLH and Product B requires 2.0 DLH. According to the current cost system, the costs to manufacture one unit of each product are:

	Product A	Product B
Direct materials	$36.00	$30.00
Direct labor	17.50	14.00
Manufacturing overhead		
2.5 DLH X $18/DLH	45.00	
2.0 DLH X $18/DLH		36.00
Total cost per unit	$98.50	$80.00

Suppose, however, that overhead costs are actually caused by the five activities listed below:

Activity	Traceable Cost
Machine setups	$255,000
Quality inspections . .	160,000
Production orders . . .	81,000
Machine-hours worked .	314,000
Material receipts	90,000
Total	$900,000

ACTIVITY-BASED COSTING EXAMPLE (cont'd)

Also suppose the following transaction data has been collected:

Activity	Number of Events or Transactions		
	Total	Product A	Product B
Machine setups	5,000	3,000	2,000
Quality inspections . . .	8,000	5,000	3,000
Production orders . . .	600	200	400
Machine-hours worked .	40,000	12,000	28,000
Material receipts	750	150	600

These data can be used to develop overhead rates for each of the five activities:

Activity	Costs	Trans-actions	Rate per Transaction
Machine setups . . .	$255,000	5,000	$51/setup
Quality inspections . .	160,000	8,000	$20/inspection
Production orders . .	81,000	600	$135/order
Machine-hours worked	314,000	40,000	$7.85/hour
Material receipts . . .	90,000	750	$120/receipt

ACTIVITY-BASED COSTING EXAMPLE (cont'd)

The overhead rates developed on the previous transparency can now be used to assign overhead costs to products:

Product A

Activity	Rate	Transactions	Amount
Machine setups	$51.00	3,000	$153,000
Quality inspections . .	20.00	5,000	100,000
Production orders . . .	135.00	200	27,000
Machine-hours worked .	7.85	12,000	94,200
Material receipts	120.00	150	18,000
Total overhead (a) . . .			$392,200
Number of units (b) . .			4,000
Overhead per unit (a) ÷ (b)			$98.05

Product B

Activity	Rate	Transactions	Amount
Machine setups	$51.00	2,000	$102,000
Quality inspections . .	20.00	3,000	60,000
Production orders . . .	135.00	400	54,000
Machine-hours worked .	7.85	28,000	219,800
Material receipts	120.00	600	72,000
Total overhead (a) . . .			$507,800
Number of units (b) . .			20,000
Overhead per unit (a) ÷ (b)			$25.39

ACTIVITY-BASED COSTING EXAMPLE (cont'd)

Product costs computed using the two different methods can now be contrasted:

Product costs using activity-based costing:

	Product A	Product B
Direct materials	$36.00	$30.00
Direct labor	17.50	14.00
Manufacturing overhead . . .	98.05	25.39
Total cost per unit	$151.55	$69.39

Product costs using the old costing system:

	Product A	Product B
Direct materials	$36.00	$30.00
Direct labor	17.50	14.00
Manufacturing overhead . . .	45.00	36.00
Total cost per unit	$98.50	$80.00

Adopting activity-based costing usually results in a shift of overhead costs from high volume to low volume products.

- **The per unit costs of the low volume products increase and the per unit costs of the high volume products decrease.**

- **The effects are not symmetrical — there is a bigger dollar effect on the per unit costs of the low volume products.**

VARIABLE COST BEHAVIOR

Three cost behavior patterns—variable, fixed, and mixed—are commonly found in organizations.

A <u>variable cost</u> changes in total in direct proportion to changes in the level of activity; a variable cost is constant on a per-unit basis.

For example, suppose each bicycle that is produced requires one bicycle chain costing $8.

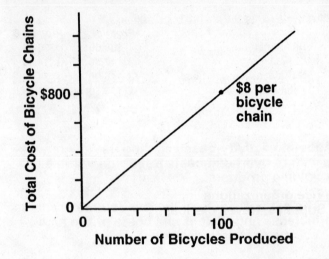

EXAMPLES OF COSTS THAT ARE NORMALLY VARIABLE WITH RESPECT TO VOLUME

Merchandising company
Costs of goods (merchandise) sold

Manufacturing company
Manufacturing costs:
Prime costs:
Direct materials
Direct labor
Variable portion of manufacturing overhead:
Indirect materials
Lubricants
Supplies
Power
Setup
Indirect labor

Both merchandising and manufacturing companies
Selling, general, and administrative costs:
Commissions
Clerical costs, such as invoicing
Shipping costs

Service organizations
Supplies, travel, clerical

CURVILINEAR COSTS
AND THE RELEVANT RANGE

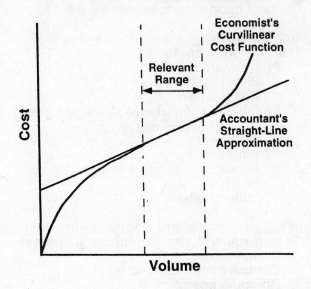

FIXED COST BEHAVIOR

EXAMPLES OF FIXED COSTS

• <u>Committed fixed costs</u>. These costs relate to investment in plant, equipment, and the basic administrative structure of a firm. Committed fixed costs are long-term in nature and usually continue without much change even in times of economic difficulty. Examples of committed fixed costs include:
   • Depreciation on plant facilities.
   • Taxes on real estate.
   • Insurance.
   • Salaries of key operating personnel.

• <u>Discretionary fixed costs</u>. These costs arise from annual decisions by management to spend specific amounts in certain areas. Examples of discretionary fixed costs include:
   • Advertising.
   • Research.
   • Management development programs.

TREND TOWARD FIXED COSTS

The trend is toward greater fixed costs relative to variable costs. The reasons for this trend are:
   • Increase in automation of facilities.
   • Movement toward stabilized employment.

FIXED COST PATTERNS

A <u>fixed cost</u> remains constant in total amount throughout wide ranges of activity.

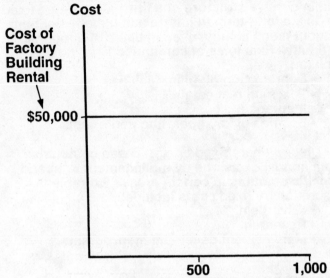

FIXED COST PATTERNS (cont'd)

A fixed cost varies inversely with activity if expressed on a per unit basis.

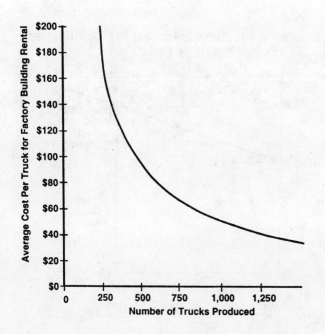

MIXED COST BEHAVIOR
AND ANALYSIS

A <u>mixed (or semivariable) cost</u> is one that
contains both variable and fixed cost elements.

Example: A machine is leased for $25,000 per
year plus 10¢ per machine hour.

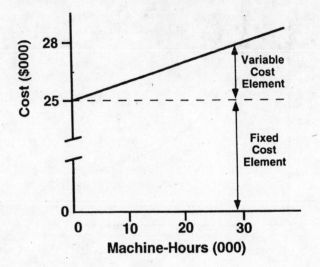

MIXED COST BEHAVIOR AND ANALYSIS (cont'd)

A cost that is considered fixed in one firm might be considered variable or semi-variable in another firm.

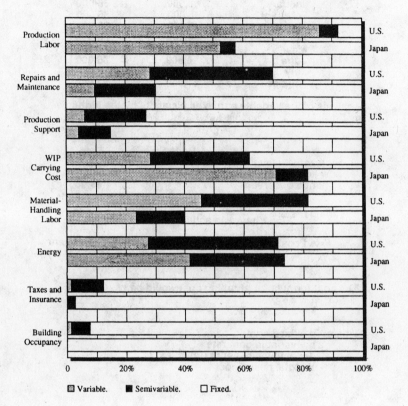

HIGH-LOW METHOD

EXAMPLE: Kohler Company has incurred shipping costs as follows over the past eight months:

Month	Units Sold	Shipping Cost
January	6,000	$ 66,000
February	5,000	65,000
March	7,000	70,000
April	9,000	80,000
May	8,000	76,000
June	10,000	85,000
July	12,000	100,000
August	11,000	87,000

Analysis of the variable and fixed elements by the high-low method:

	Units Sold	Shipping Cost
High activity level	12,000	$100,000
Low activity level	5,000	65,000
Change observed	7,000	$ 35,000

$$\text{Variable rate} = \frac{\text{Change in cost}}{\text{Change in activity}} = \frac{\$35,000}{7,000 \text{ units}} = \$5/\text{Unit}$$

Fixed cost element = Total cost - Variable cost element
= $100,000 - (12,000 units X $5/unit)
= $40,000

The cost formula for shipping cost would be:
Y = a + bX
Y = $40,000 + $5X

where: a = fixed cost
b = variable cost rate
X = activity measure (units, etc.)
Y = total mixed cost

EVALUATION OF THE HIGH-LOW METHOD

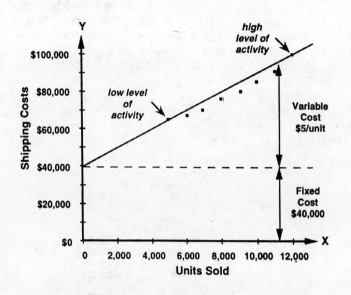

The high-low method suffers from two major defects. Generally, two points are not enough to produce accurate results <u>and</u> the high and low volume periods are often unusual.

SCATTERGRAPH METHOD

In the <u>scattergraph method</u>, a line is fitted to the plotted points by eye using a ruler. Ordinarily the scattergraph method is a better way of determining a cost formula than the high-low method. The scattergraph method includes all of the observed cost data in the analysis.

Example: Piedmont Company has maintained records of the number of orders and billing costs in each quarter over the past several years.

Quarter	Number of Orders	Billing Costs
19x1—1st	1,500	$42,000
2nd	1,900	46,000
3rd	1,000	37,000
4th	1,300	43,000
19x2—1 st	2,800	54,000
2nd	1,700	47,000
3rd	2,100	51,000
4th	1,100	42,000
19x3—1 st	2,000	48,000
2nd	2,400	53,000
3rd	2,300	49,000

The line fitted to the plotted data is called a <u>regression line</u>. Typically, the regression line is placed so that approximately equal numbers of points fall above and below it. Subsequent calculations are also a little easier if the regression line is drawn through one of the points.

A COMPLETED SCATTERGRAPH

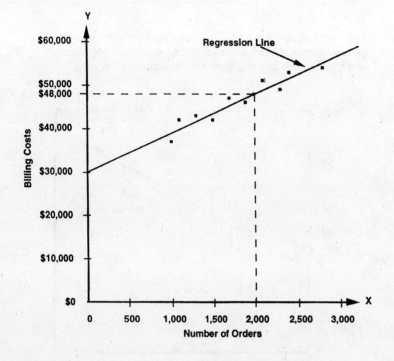

Select a point falling on the line (in this case 2,000 orders):

Total billing cost for 2,000 orders $48,000
Less fixed cost element   30,000
Variable cost element $18,000

$18,000 ÷ 2,000 orders = $9/order. Therefore, Y = $30,000 + $9X.

LEAST-SQUARES METHOD

The *least squares method* for analyzing mixed costs uses mathematical formulas to compute the regression line that minimizes the sum of the squared "errors."

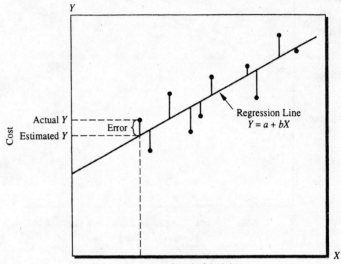

Since the least squares method uses methematical formulas to compute the regression line, this method is more objective and precise than the scattergraph method which relies on fitting a line by eye.

LEAST SQUARES METHOD (cont'd)

Example: Montrose Hospital operates a small cafeteria and management is interested in the relationship between cafeteria costs and the number of meals served.

Month	Meals Served (000) (X)	Total Cost (Y)	XY	X^2
April	4	$ 9,500	$ 38,000	16
May	1	4,000	4,000	1
June	3	8,000	24,000	9
July	5	10,000	50,000	25
August	10	19,500	195,000	100
September	7	14,000	98,000	49
	30	$65,000	$409,000	200

The calculations illustrated below are explained in detail in the appendix to Chapter 6.

(1) $\sum XY = a\sum X + b\sum X^2$ $409,000 = 30a + 200b$
(2) $\sum Y = na + b\sum X$ $ 65,000 = 6a + 30b$

(1) $409,000 = 30a + 200b$
(2) Multiply by 5: $325,000 = 30a + 150b$
Subtract (2) from (1): $84,000 = 50b$
Divide by 50: $ 1,680 = b$

Therefore, the variable rate is $1,680 per thousand meals or $1.68 per meal.

Substitute in equation (2): $65,000 = 6a + 30($1,680)
                          $65,000 = 6a + $50,400
Subtract $50,400 $14,600 = 6a
Divide by 6 $2,433 = a (rounded)

The cost formula is: Y = $2,433 per month + $1.68 per meal.

CONTRIBUTION INCOME STATEMENT VS. TRADITIONAL INCOME STATEMENT
(Exhibit 6-12)

Traditional Approach			*Contribution Approach*		
(costs organized by function)			*(costs organized by behavior)*		
Sales		$12,000	Sales		$12,000
Less cost of goods sold		6,000*	Less variable expenses:		
Gross margin		6,000	Variable production	$2,000	
Less operating expenses:			Variable selling	600	
Selling	$3,100*		Variable administrative	400	3,000
Administrative	1,900*	5,000	Contribution margin		9,000
Net income		$1,000	Less fixed expenses:		
			Fixed production	4,000	
			Fixed selling	2,500	
			Fixed administrative	1,500	8,000
			Net income		$1,000

* Contains both variable and fixed expenses. This is the income statement for a manufacturing company. If this were the income statement for a merchandising company, then the cost of goods sold would be all variable.

OVERVIEW OF CVP ANALYSIS

<u>Cost-volume-profit (CVP) analysis</u> is concerned with the relationships among prices of products, unit volume, per unit variable costs, total fixed costs, and mix of products sold.

THE CONTRIBUTION APPROACH

A contribution income statement is very useful in CVP analysis. A contribution income statement for the Nord Company, a manufacturer of exercise bicycles, for last month follows:

	Total	Per Unit	Percent
Sales (500 bikes)	$250,000	$500	100%
Less variable expenses .	150,000	300	60
Contribution margin . . .	100,000	$200	40%
Less fixed expenses . . .	80,000		
Net income	$ 20,000		

CONTRIBUTION MARGIN:

- The amount that sales (net of variable expenses) contributes toward covering fixed expenses and then toward profits.

- The per unit contribution margin remains constant so long as the selling price and the variable expense per unit do not change.

VOLUME CHANGES AND NET INCOME

Contribution income statements are given on this and the following transparency for monthly sales of 1, 2, 400, and 401 bikes.

	Total	Per Unit	Percent
Sales (*1 bike*)	$500	$500	100%
Less variable expenses .	300	300	60
Contribution margin	200	$200	. 40%
Less fixed expenses . .	80,000		
Net income (loss) . . .	$(79,800)		

	Total	Per Unit	Percent
Sales (*2 bikes*)	$1,000	$500	100%
Less variable expenses .	600	300	60
Contribution margin	400	$200	40%
Less fixed expenses . .	80,000		
Net income (loss) . . .	$(79,600)		

Note the following points:

1. The contribution margin must first cover the fixed expenses. If the contribution margin is not sufficient to cover the fixed expenses, then a loss occurs for the period.

2. As additional units are sold, the fixed expenses are whittled down little by little until they have all been covered.

VOLUME CHANGES AND NET INCOME (cont'd)

	Total	Per Unit	Percent
Sales (400 bikes) . . .	$200,000	$500	100%
Less variable expenses	120,000	300	60
Contribution margin . . .	80,000	$200	40%
Less fixed expenses . .	80,000		
Net income	$ -0-		

	Total	Per Unit	Percent
Sales (401 bikes) . . .	$200,500	$500	100%
Less variable expenses	120,300	300	60
Contribution margin . . .	80,200	$200	40%
Less fixed expenses . .	80,000		
Net income	$ 200		

Note the following points:

1. If the company sells exactly 400 bikes a month, it will just break even (no profit or loss).

2. The **break-even point** can be defined either as:
   - The point where total sales revenue equals total expenses (variable and fixed).
   - The point where total contribution margin equals total fixed expenses.

3. Once the break-even point is reached, net income increases by amount of the unit contribution margin for each additional unit sold.

CONTRIBUTION MARGIN RATIO

The <u>contribution margin (CM) ratio</u> is the ratio of contribution margin to total sales expressed as a percentage. The CM ratio is computed as follows:

$$\frac{\text{Contribution margin}}{\text{Total sales}} = \text{CM ratio}$$

The CM ratio can also be computed using per unit figures as follows:

$$\frac{\text{Unit contribution margin}}{\text{Per unit price}} = \text{CM ratio}$$

EXAMPLE: For Nord company, the CM ratio is 40%, computed as follows:

$$\frac{\text{Contribution margin}}{\text{Total sales}} = \frac{\$100,000}{\$250,000} = 40\%$$

or

$$\frac{\text{Unit contribution margin}}{\text{Per unit price}} = \frac{\$200}{\$500} = 40\%$$

See 7-1

CONTRIBUTION MARGIN RATIO (cont'd)

The CM ratio shows how the contribution margin will be affected by a given change in total sales.

EXAMPLE: Assume that sales in Nord Company increase by $150,000 next month. What will be the effect on (1) the contribution margin and (2) the net income?

(1) Effect on contribution margin:

Increase in sales	$150,000
Multiply by the CM ratio	X 40%
Increase in contribution margin . .	$ 60,000

(2) Effect on net income:

If the fixed expenses do not change, the net income for the month will also increase by $60,000.

Verification:

	Present	Expected	Change
Sales (in units)	500	800	300
Sales (in dollars)	$250,000	$400,000	$150,000
Less variable expenses	150,000	240,000	90,000
Contribution margin	100,000	160,000	60,000
Less fixed expenses	80,000	80,000	-0-
Net income	$ 20,000	$ 80,000	$ 60,000

BREAK-EVEN ANALYSIS

To demonstrate break-even analysis, we will continue to use data for the Nord Company:

	Per Bike	Percent
Selling price	$500	100%
Variable expenses	300	60
Contribution margin	$200	40%

Fixed expenses are $80,000 per month.

EQUATION METHOD

X = Break-even point in bikes.
Sales = Variable Expenses + Fixed Expenses + Profits
$500X = $300X + $80,000 + $0
$200X = $80,000
X = 400 bikes
(or, in terms of total sales dollars, $500 x 400 = $200,000)

X = Break-even point in sales dollars.
Sales = Variable Expenses + Fixed Expenses + Profits
X = 0.60X + $80,000 + $0
0.40X = $80,000
X = $200,000

CONTRIBUTION METHOD

$$\text{Break-even in units} = \frac{\text{Fixed expenses}}{\text{Unit contribution margin}}$$
$$= \frac{\$80,000}{\$200} = 400 \text{ bikes}$$

$$\text{Break-even in sales dollars} = \frac{\text{Fixed expenses}}{\text{CM ratio}}$$
$$= \frac{\$80,000}{0.40} = \$200,000$$

PREPARING A CVP GRAPH

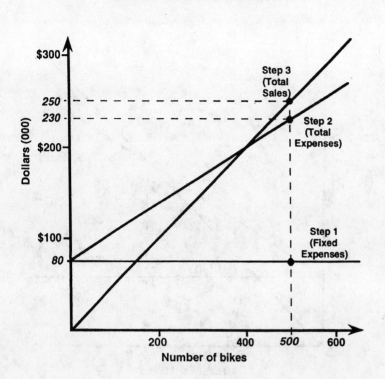

THE COMPLETED CVP GRAPH

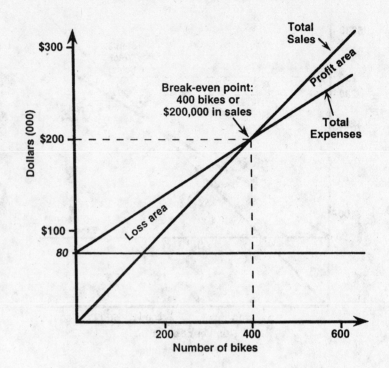

AN ALTERNATE FORMAT FOR THE CVP GRAPH

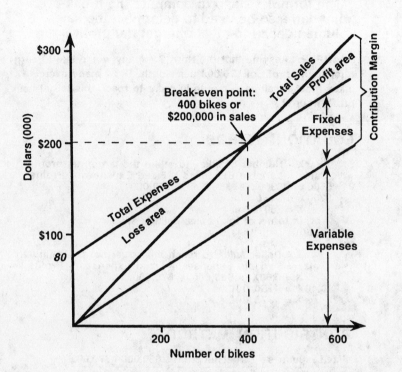

TARGET NET PROFIT ANALYSIS

The formulas used to compute the break-even point can also be used to determine the sales volume needed to meet a target net profit figure.

EXAMPLE: Assume that the Nord Company would like to earn a minimum profit of $70,000 per month. How many exercise bikes must it sell each month in order to reach this target net profit figure?

EQUATION METHOD

X = Number of bikes to attain the target net profit.
Sales = Variable Expenses + Fixed Expenses + Profits
$\$500X = \$300X + \$80,000 + \$70,000$
$\$200X = \$150,000$
$X = 750$ Bikes
(or, in terms of total sales dollars, $500 x 750 = $375,000)

X = Dollar sales to reach the target net profit figure.
Sales = Variable Expenses + Fixed Expenses + Profits
$X = 0.60X + \$80,000 + \$70,000$
$0.40X = \$150,000$
$X = \$375,000$

CONTRIBUTION METHOD

$$\frac{\text{Fixed expenses} + \text{Target net profit}}{\text{Unit contribution margin}} = \frac{\$80,000 + \$70,000}{\$200} = 750 \text{ bikes}$$

$$\frac{\text{Fixed expenses} + \text{Target net profit}}{\text{CM ratio}} = \frac{\$80,000 + \$70,000}{0.40} = \$375,000$$

MARGIN OF SAFETY

The <u>margin of safety</u> (MS) is the excess of budgeted (or actual) sales over the break-even sales. It shows the amount by which sales can drop before losses begin to be incurred.

The margin of safety can be expressed either in dollar form or in percentage form. The formulas are:

**Total Sales — Break-Even Sales
= Margin of Safety (in dollars)**

**Margin of Safety (in dollars) ÷ Total Sales
= Margin of Safety (In percent)**

	Company X		Company Y	
Sales	$500,000	100%	$500,000	100%
Less variable expenses	350,000	70	100,000	20
Contribution margin	150,000	30%	400,000	80%
Less fixed expenses	90,000		340,000	
Net income	$ 60,000		$ 60,000	

Break-even point:
$90,000 ÷ .30 $300,000
$340,000 ÷ .80 $425,000

MS in dollars:
$500,000 — $300,000 $200,000
$500,000 — $425,000 $75,000

MS in percent:
$200,000 ÷ $500,000   40%
$75,000 ÷ $500,000   15%

OPERATING LEVERAGE

Operating leverage is a measure of the mix of variable and fixed costs in a firm. The formula to compute the degree of operating leverage at a given level of sales is:

$$\frac{\text{Contribution Margin}}{\text{Net Income}} = \text{Degree of Operating Leverage}$$

	Company X		Company Y	
Sales	$500,000	100%	$500,000	100%
Less variable expenses	350,000	70	100,000	20
Contribution margin	150,000	30%	400,000	80%
Less fixed expenses	90,000		340,000	
Net income	$ 60,000		$ 60,000	
Degree of Operating Leverage	2.5		6.7	

The degree of operating leverage can be used to predict the impact on net income of a given percentage increase in sales. For example, if the degree of operating leverage is 2.5 and there is a 10% increase in sales, then net income will increase by 25% (= 2.5 x 10%).

EXAMPLE: Assume that both company X and Y experience a 10 percent increase in sales:

	Company X		Company Y	
Sales	$550,000	100%	$550,000	100%
Less variable expenses	385,000	70	110,000	20
Contribution margin	165,000	30%	440,000	80%
Less fixed expenses	90,000		340,000	
Net income	$ 75,000		$100,000	
Increase in net income	25%		67%	

OPERATING LEVERAGE (cont'd)

Note that the degree of operating leverage is not constant—it changes with the level of sales.

EXAMPLE: At the higher level of sales, the degree of operating leverage for company X declines from 2.5 down to 2.2 and for Company Y from 6.7 down to 4.4.

	Company X (000s)		Company Y (000s)	
Sales	$500	$550	$500	$550
Less variable expenses	350	385	100	110
Contribution margin	150	165	400	440
Less fixed expenses	90	90	340	340
Net income	$ 60	$ 75	$ 60	$100
Degree of operating leverage	2.5	2.2	6.7	4.4

Ordinarily, the degree of operating leverage declines as sales increase.

COMPARISON OF CAPITAL-INTENSIVE AND LABOR-INTENSIVE COMPANIES

The comparison below is between two companies in the same industry that produce identical products for the same market. One of the companies has chosen to automate its facilities (capital intensive) and the other has chosen to rely heavily on direct labor inputs (labor intensive).

Item	Capital-Intensive (automated) Company	Labor-Intensive Company	Comments
The CM ratio for a given product will tend to be relatively . . .	High	Low	Variable costs in an automated company will tend to be lower than in a labor-intensive company, thereby causing the CM ratio for a given product to be higher.
Operating leverage will tend to be . . .	High	Low	Since operating leverage is a measure of the use of fixed costs in an organization, it will typically be higher in an automated company than in a company that relies on direct labor inputs.
In periods of increasing sales, net income will tend to increase . . .	Rapidly	Slowly	Since both operating leverage and product CM ratios tend to be high in automated companies, net income will increase rapidly after the break-even point has been reached.
In periods of decreasing sales, net income will tend to decrease . . .	Rapidly	Slowly	Just as net income increases rapidly in an automated company after the break-even point has been reached, so will net income decrease rapidly as sales decrease.
The volatility of net income with changes in sales will tend to be . . .	Greater	Less	Due to its higher operating leverage, the net income in an automated company will tend to be much more sensitive to changes in sales than in a labor-intensive company.
The break-even point will tend to be . . .	Higher	Lower	The break-even point in an automated company will tend to be higher because of its greater fixed costs.
The MS at a given level of sales will tend to be...	Lower	Higher	The MS in an automated company will tend to be lower because of its higher break-even point.
The latitude available to management in times of economic stress will tend to be . . .	Less	Greater	With high fixed costs in an automated company, management is more "locked in" and has fewer options when dealing with changing economic conditions.
The overall degree of risk associated with operating activities will tend to be . . .	Greater	Less	The risk factor is a summation of all the other factors listed above.

MULTI-PRODUCT BREAK-EVEN ANALYSIS

When there are multiple products, break-even analysis can be easily accomplished using the <u>overall contribution margin ratio</u>.

$$\text{Overall contribution margin ratio} = \frac{\text{Total contribution margin}}{\text{Total sales dollars}}$$

	Product A		Product B		Total	
Sales	$100,000	100%	$300,000	100%	$400,000	100.0%
Less variable expenses	70,000	70	120,000	40	190,000	47.5
Contribution margin	$ 30,000	30%	$180,000	60%	210,000	52.5%
Less fixed expenses					141,750	
Net income					$ 68,250	

$$\text{Overall contribution margin ratio} = \frac{\text{Total contribution margin}}{\text{Total sales dollars}} = \frac{\$210,000}{\$400,000} = 52.5\%$$

$$\text{Break-even in sales dollars} = \frac{\text{Fixed expenses}}{\text{Overall CM ratio}} = \frac{\$141,750}{0.525} = \$270,000$$

MULTI-PRODUCT BREAK-EVEN ANALYSIS (cont'd)

Note: If the proportions in which the products are sold (i.e., "the sales mix") changes, then the overall contribution margin ratio will change.

Example: Assume that total sales remain unchanged at $400,000. However, there is a shift in the sales mix so that the mix is the reverse of what it was in the prior example.

	Product A		Product B		Total	
Sales	$300,000	100%	$100,000	100%	$400,000	100.0%
Less variable expenses	210,000	70	40,000	40	250,000	62.5
Contribution margin	$ 90,000	30%	$ 60,000	60%	150,000	37.5%
Less fixed expenses					141,750	
Net income					$ 8,250	

$$\text{Overall contribution margin ratio} = \frac{\text{Total contribution margin}}{\text{Total sales dollars}} = \frac{\$150,000}{\$400,000} = 37.5\%$$

$$\text{Break-even in sales dollars} = \frac{\text{Fixed expenses}}{\text{Overall CM ratio}} = \frac{\$141,750}{0.375} = \$378,000$$

ASSUMPTIONS OF CVP ANALYSIS

1. The behavior of both revenue and costs is linear. Revenue is strictly proportional to volume (i.e., the selling price is constant) and cost is a linear function of volume.

2. Costs can be accurately divided into variable and fixed elements.

3. The sales mix is constant in multi-product firms.

4. Inventories do not change. The number of units produced equals the number of units sold.

5. Worker and machine productivities don't change.

6. The value of a dollar received today is the same as the value of a dollar received in the future.

VARIABLE VERSUS ABSORPTION COSTING

VARIABLE COSTING

Under <u>variable costing</u>, only those costs of production that vary directly with volume are treated as product costs.
- These costs usually consist of direct materials, direct labor, and variable manufacturing overhead.
- Fixed manufacturing overhead is not treated as a product cost under variable costing. Rather, it is treated as a period cost and deducted in full each year from revenues.
- Variable costing may be used by companies internally for planning and for controlling operations. However, variable costing is not acceptable for tax reporting and audited external reports.

ABSORPTION COSTING

<u>Absorption costing</u> treats <u>all</u> costs of production as product costs.
- The cost of a unit of product under the absorption costing method consists of direct materials, direct labor, and both variable <u>and</u> fixed manufacturing overhead.
- Therefore, under absorption costing a portion of the fixed manufacturing overhead is allocated to each unit of product.

CLASSIFICATION OF COSTS UNDER VARIABLE AND ABSORPTION COSTING

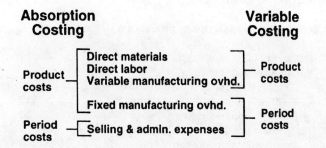

Absorption Costing

Variable Costing

Product costs
- Direct materials
- Direct labor
- Variable manufacturing ovhd.
→ Product costs

- Fixed manufacturing ovhd.

Period costs
- Selling & admin. expenses
→ Period costs

UNIT COST COMPUTATIONS

Unit product costs differ between variable and absorption costing.

EXAMPLE: Harvey Company produces a single product.

Number of units produced annually	25,000
Variable costs per unit:	
Direct materials, direct labor, and	
variable manufacturing overhead	$10
Selling & administrative expense	$3
Fixed costs per year:	
Manufacturing overhead	$150,000
Selling & administrative expense	$100,000

The cost of a single unit of product under the two costing methods would be:

	Absorption Costing	Variable Costing
Direct materials, direct labor, and		
variable manufacturing overhead . . .	$10	$10
Fixed manufacturing overhead		
($150,000÷25,000 units)	6	-
Total cost per unit	$16	$10

Note that selling and administrative expenses are not treated as product costs under either costing method. Selling and administrative expenses are always treated as period costs and deducted from revenues as incurred.

INCOME COMPARISON

Harvey Company had no beginning inventory, produced 25,000 units, and sold 20,000 units last year.

Absorption costing

Sales (20,000 units x $30)		$600,000
Less cost of goods sold:		
Beginning inventory	$ -0-	
Add COGM (25,000 units x $16)	400,000	
Goods available for sale	400,000	
Ending inventory (5,000 units x $16) . . .	80,000	320,000
Gross margin		280,000
Less selling & admin. expense (Variable:		
20,000 units x $3; Fixed: $100,000)		160,000
Net income		$120,000

Variable costing

Sales (20,000 units x $30)		$600,000
Less variable expenses:		
Variable cost of goods sold:		
Beginning inventory	$ -0-	
Variable mfg. costs (25,000 units x $10)	250,000	
Goods available for sale	250,000	
Ending inventory (5,000 units x $10) . .	50,000	
Variable cost of goods sold	200,000	
Variable selling & admin. expense		
(20,000 units x $3)	60,000	260,000
Contribution margin		340,000
Less fixed expenses:		
Manufacturing overhead	150,000	
Selling & admin. expense	100,000	250,000
Net income		$ 90,000

INCOME COMPARISON (cont'd)

	Cost of Goods Sold	Ending Inventory	Period Expense	Total
Absorption costing				
Variable mfg. costs	$200,000	$50,000	-	$250,000
Fixed mfg. overhead	120,000	30,000	-	150,000
	$320,000	$80,000	-	$400,000
Variable costing				
Variable mfg. costs	$200,000	$50,000	-	$250,000
Fixed mfg. overhead	-	-	$150,000	150,000
	$200,000	$50,000	$150,000	$400,000

EXTENDED INCOME COMPARISON

EXAMPLE: Holland Company produces a single product.

Number of units produced annually	5,000
Variable costs per unit:	
Direct materials, direct labor, and	
variable manufacturing overhead	$5
Selling & administrative expense	$1
Fixed costs per year:	
Manufacturing overhead	$15,000
Selling & admin. expense	$21,000

The cost of a single unit of product under the two costing methods would be:

	Absorption Costing	Variable Costing
Direct materials, direct labor, and		
variable manufacturing overhead . . .	$5	$5
Fixed manufacturing overhead		
($15,000 ÷ 5,000 units)	<u>3</u>	<u>-</u>
Total cost per unit	<u>$8</u>	<u>$5</u>

Income statements using each of the two costing methods over a three-year period are provided on the following transparency. (Note the computation of the variable cost of goods sold on the variable costing income statements. The method used is simpler than the method used in the previous example.)

EXTENDED INCOME COMPARISON (cont'd)

	Year 1	Year 2	Year 3	Total
Units produced	5,000	5,000	5,000	15,000
Units sold	5,000	4,000	6,000	15,000

Absorption costing

	Year 1	Year 2	Year 3	Total
Sales (@ $15)	$75,000	$60,000	$90,000	$225,000
Less cost of goods sold:				
Beginning inventory (@ $8)	-0-	-0-	8,000	-0-
COGM (@ $8)	40,000	40,000	40,000	120,000
Goods available for sale	40,000	40,000	48,000	120,000
Ending inventory (@ $8)	-0-	8,000	-0-	-0-
Cost of goods sold	40,000	32,000	48,000	120,000
Gross margin	35,000	28,000	42,000	105,000
Less selling & admin.	26,000	25,000	27,000	78,000
Net income	$ 9,000	$ 3,000	$15,000	$27,000

Variable costing

	Year 1	Year 2	Year 3	Total
Sales (@ $15)	$75,000	$60,000	$90,000	$225,000
Less variable expenses:				
Variable COGS (@ $5)	25,000	20,000	30,000	75,000
Variable selling & admin. expenses (@ $1)	5,000	4,000	6,000	15,000
Total variable expenses	30,000	24,000	36,000	90,000
Contribution margin	45,000	36,000	54,000	135,000
Less fixed expenses:				
Manufacturing overhead	15,000	15,000	15,000	45,000
Selling & admin. expense	21,000	21,000	21,000	63,000
Total fixed expenses	36,000	36,000	36,000	108,000
Net income	$ 9,000	$ -0-	$18,000	$ 27,000

EXTENDED INCOME COMPARISON (cont'd)

A reconciliation of the net income figures for the two methods over the three year period follows:

	Year 1	Year 2	Year 3
Variable costing net income	$9,000	$ -0-	$18,000
Add: Fixed overhead cost deferred in inventory under absorption costing (1,000 units x $3)	—	3,000	—
Deduct: Fixed overhead cost released from inventory under absorption costing (1,000 units x $3)	—	—	(3,000)
Absorption costing net income	$9,000	$3,000	$15,000

COMPARATIVE INCOME EFFECTS —
VARIABLE AND ABSORPTION COSTING

Relationship Between Production and Sales	As Compared to the Other Costing Method, Net Income Tends to Be ...	
	Variable Costing	Absorption Costing
Production = sales	Same	Same
Production > sales	Lower	Higher*
Production < sales	Higher	Lower#

* Net income will tend to be higher since fixed overhead cost will be *deferred* in inventory under absorption costing.

\# Net income will tend to be lower since fixed overhead cost will be *released* from inventory under absorption costing.

JIT AND ABSORPTION COSTING

- Under JIT, finished goods and work-in-process inventories are reduced to a minimum.

- Therefore, under JIT discrepancies between production and sales are reduced — sometimes to negligible levels. Since there are little or no inventories under JIT, opportunities to defer fixed overhead in inventories are reduced or eliminated.

- As a consequence, the difference between absorption and variable costing net incomes may be reduced to negligible levels under JIT.

- Also, JIT will reduce or eliminate the sometimes erratic movement of net income under absorption costing. For example, under JIT, it is less likely that absorption costing income will move in the opposite direction to sales due to a buildup in inventories.

OVERVIEW OF BUDGETING

A <u>budget</u> is a detailed plan for the acquisition and use of financial and other resources over a specified time period. The budgeting process involves two stages:

- **Planning, which includes developing future objectives and preparing various detailed budgets to achieve those objectives.**

- **Control, which involves the steps taken by management to ensure that the objectives set down at the planning stage are attained.**

ADVANTAGES OF BUDGETING

- **Budgeting requires that managers give planning top priority, and it provides managers with a way to formalize their planning.**

- **Budgeting is a vehicle for communicating plans throughout the organization.**

- **Budgeting provides definite goals that serve as benchmarks for evaluating subsequent performance.**

- **Budgeting uncovers potential bottlenecks.**

- **Budgeting coordinates the activities of the entire organization.**

TYPES OF BUDGETS

The <u>master budget</u> is a summary of all phases of a company's plans and goals for the future.

- It sets specific targets for sales, production, material purchases, and financing activities.

- It culminates in projected statements of net income, financial position, and cash flows.

The master budget can be divided into two major parts—capital budgets and operating budgets.

- <u>Capital budgets</u> cover acquisition of land, buildings, and other items of capital equipment, and have time horizons that may extend many years into the future.

- <u>Operating budgets</u> cover sales, production, material purchases, cash and related areas.
  - These budgets usually have a time horizon of one year.
  - Operating budgets may be prepared on a continuous or perpetual basis.

MASTER BUDGET INTERRELATIONSHIPS
(EXHIBIT 9-2)

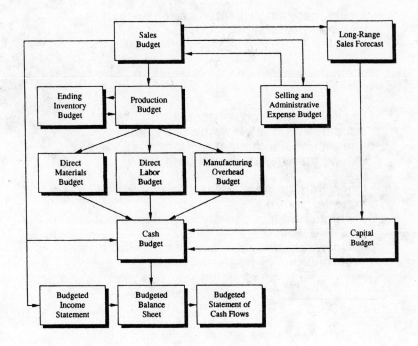

BUDGETING EXAMPLE

Royal Company is preparing budgets for the quarter ended June 30.

- Budgeted sales for the next five months are:

April	20,000 units
May	50,000 units
June	30,000 units
July	25,000 units
August	15,000 units

- The selling price is $10 per unit.

- The following budgets will be prepared in this example:
  - Sales budget (with a schedule of expected cash collections).
  - Production budget.
  - Material purchases budget (with a schedule of expected cash payments).
  - Direct labor budget.
  - Manufacturing overhead budget.
  - Selling and administrative expense budget.
  - Cash budget.

SALES BUDGET

	April	May	June	Quarter
Budgeted sales (units)	20,000	50,000	30,000	100,000
Selling price per unit	X $10	X $10	X $10	X $10
Budgeted sales (dollars)	$200,000	$500,000	$300,000	$1,000,000

SCHEDULE OF EXPECTED CASH COLLECTIONS

All sales are on account. The company's collection pattern is: 70% collected in the month of sale; 25% collected in the month following sale; and the remaining 5% is uncollectible. The accounts receivable balance on March 31 was $30,000 and all of this was collectible.

	April	May	June	Quarter
Accounts receivable:				
March 31	$ 30,000			$ 30,000
April sales:				
70% X $200,000 . . .	140,000			140,000
25% X $200,000 . . .		$ 50,000		50,000
May sales:				
70% X $500,000 . . .		350,000		350,000
25% X $500,000 . . .			$125,000	125,000
June sales:				
70% X $300,000 . . .			210,000	210,000
Total cash collections .	$170,000	$400,000	$335,000	$905,000

PRODUCTION BUDGET

The company desires to have inventory on hand at the end of each month equal to 20 percent of the following month's budgeted sales in units. On March 31, 4,000 units were on hand.

	April	May	June	July
Sales in units	20,000	50,000	30,000	25,000
Add desired ending				
inventory	10,000	6,000	5,000	3,000
Total needs	30,000	56,000	35,000	28,000
Less beginning				
inventory	4,000	10,000	6,000	5,000
Production in units . . .	26,000	46,000	29,000	23,000

MATERIAL PURCHASES BUDGET

Five pounds of material are required per unit of product. The company desires to have materials on hand at the end of each month equal to 10 percent of the following month's production needs. The beginning materials inventory was 13,000 lbs.

	April	May	June	Quarter
Production in units . . .	26,000	46,000	29,000	101,000
Materials per unit (lbs.) .	X 5	X 5	X 5	X 5
Production needs (lbs.) .	130,000	230,000	145,000	505,000
Add desired ending inventory (lbs.)	23,000	14,500	11,500*	11,500
Total needs (lbs.)	153,000	244,500	156,500	516,500
Less beginning inventory (lbs.)	13,000	23,000	14,500	13,000
Material to be purchased (lbs.) . . .	140,000	221,500	142,000	503,500

* 23,000 units in July X 5 lbs. = 115,000 lbs.
115,000 lbs. X 10% = 11,500 lbs.

SCHEDULE OF EXPECTED CASH PAYMENTS FOR MATERIAL

The material used in production costs $0.40 per pound. One-half of a month's purchases are paid for in the month of purchase; the other half is paid for in the following month. No discount terms are available. The accounts payable balance on March 31 was $12,000.

	April	May	June	Quarter
Material purchases (lbs.)	140,000	221,500	142,000	503,500
Cost per lb.	X $0.40	X $0.40	X $0.40	X $0.40
Total cost of purchases	$ 56,000	$ 88,600	$ 56,800	$201,400
Accounts payable:				
March 31	$12,000			$ 12,000
April purchases:				
50% X $56,000	28,000			28,000
50% X $56,000		$28,000		28,000
May purchases:				
50% X $88,600		44,300		44,300
50% X $88,600			$44,300	44,300
June purchases:				
50% X $56,800			28,400	28,400
Total cash payments				
for materials	$40,000	$72,300	$72,700	$185,000

DIRECT LABOR BUDGET

Each unit produced requires 0.05 hour of direct labor. Royal has a "no layoff" policy and in effect guarantees its direct labor employees that they will be paid for at least 40 hours per week at the normal rate of $10 per hour. In exchange for this guarantee, the direct labor workforce has agreed to work overtime when required at the same rate of $10 per hour. In each of the months of April, May and June, the direct labor workforce has been guaranteed a total of 1,500 paid hours.

	April	May	June	Quarter
Production in units . . .	26,000	46,000	29,000	101,000
Direct labor hours per unit	X 0.05	X 0.05	X 0.05	X 0.05
Labor hours required . .	1,300	2,300	1,450	5,050
Guaranteed minimum labor hours paid . . .	1,500	1,500	1,500	
Labor hours required . .	1,300	2,300	1,450	
Labor hours paid*	1,500	2,300	1,500	5,300
Wage rate	X $10	X $10	X $10	X $10
Total direct labor cost . .	$15,000	$23,000	$15,000	$53,000

* If the labor hours required for production are less than the guaranteed minimum labor hours, the workers are paid for the guaranteed minimum number of hours. Thus the labor hours paid is the larger of the guaranteed minimum and the labor hours actually required for the month's production.

MANUFACTURING OVERHEAD BUDGET

Variable manufacturing overhead is $1 per unit produced and fixed manufacturing overhead is $50,000 per month. The fixed manufacturing overhead figure includes $20,000 in costs—primarily depreciation—that are not current cash outflows.

	April	May	June	Quarter
Production in units . . .	26,000	46,000	29,000	101,000
Variable manufacturing overhead rate	X $1	X $1	X $1	X $1
Variable manufacturing overhead costs	$26,000	$46,000	$29,000	$101,000
Fixed manufacturing overhead costs	50,000	50,000	50,000	150,000
Total manufacturing overhead costs	76,000	96,000	79,000	251,000
Less noncash costs . . .	20,000	20,000	20,000	60,000
Cash disbursements for mfg. overhead	$56,000	$76,000	$59,000	$191,000

SELLING AND ADMINISTRATIVE EXPENSE BUDGET

Variable selling and administrative expenses are $.50 per unit <u>sold</u> and fixed selling and administrative expenses are $70,000 per month. The fixed selling and administrative expenses include $10,000 in costs—primarily depreciation—that are not cash outflows of the current month.

	April	*May*	*June*	*Quarter*
Sales in units	20,000	50,000	30,000	100,000
Variable selling and admin. rate	<u>X $0.50</u>	<u>X $0.50</u>	<u>X $0.50</u>	<u>X $0.50</u>
Variable selling and admin. expense	$10,000	$25,000	$15,000	$ 50,000
Fixed selling and admin. expense	<u>70,000</u>	<u>70,000</u>	<u>70,000</u>	<u>210,000</u>
Total selling and admin. expense	80,000	95,000	85,000	260,000
Less noncash expenses	<u>10,000</u>	<u>10,000</u>	<u>10,000</u>	<u>30,000</u>
Cash disbursements for selling & admin.	<u>$70,000</u>	<u>$85,000</u>	<u>$75,000</u>	<u>$230,000</u>

CASH BUDGET

The following additional information has been used in preparing a cash budget for Royal Company:

1. An open line of credit is available at a local bank, which allows the company to borrow up to $75,000 per quarter.

2. Royal Company must maintain a minimum cash balance of $30,000.

3. All borrowing occurs at the beginning of a month, and all repayments occur at the end of a month.

4. Interest is paid only at the time of repayment of principal. The interest rate is 16% per year.

5. Cash dividends in the amount of $49,000 are to be paid to shareholders in April.

6. Equipment purchases of $143,700 are scheduled for May and $48,300 for June.

7. The cash balance at the beginning of April was $40,000.

A cash budget for the company, by month and for the quarter in total, is presented on the following page.

CASH BUDGET (cont'd)

	April	May	June	Quarter
Cash balance, beginning	$ 40,000	$ 30,000	$ 30,000	$ 40,000
Add receipts:				
Cash collections . . .	170,000	400,000	335,000	905,000
Total cash available . . .	210,000	430,000	365,000	945,000
Less disbursements:				
Material purchases . .	40,000	72,300	72,700	185,000
Direct labor	15,000	23,000	15,000	53,000
Mfg. overhead	56,000	76,000	59,000	191,000
Selling and admin. .	70,000	85,000	75,000	230,000
Equipment purchases	—	143,700	48,300	192,000
Dividends	49,000	—	—	49,000
Total disbursements . .	230,000	400,000	270,000	900,000
Excess (deficiency) of cash available over disbursements	(20,000)	30,000	95,000	45,000
Financing:				
Borrowing	50,000	—	—	50,000
Repayments	—	—	(50,000)	(50,000)
Interest*	—	—	(2,000)	(2,000)
Total financing	50,000	—	(52,000)	(2,000)
Cash balance, ending .	$ 30,000	$ 30,000	$ 43,000	$ 43,000

* $50,000 X 0.16 X (3/12) = $2,000.

JIT PURCHASING

There is a difference between JIT production and JIT purchasing.

- JIT production is limited to manufacturers.

- JIT purchasing can be used by any firm—retail, wholesale, distribution, or manufacturing. It focuses on the acquisition of goods.

The central thrust of JIT is simplification and elimination of waste. This thrust is evident in JIT purchasing:

1. As far as possible, goods are received from suppliers just before they are needed.

2. The number of suppliers is greatly decreased; long-term, stable relationships with a few reliable suppliers are emphasized.

3. Long-term agreements stipulate the delivery schedule, the quality, and the price.

4. There is little or no inspection of goods received from a supplier.

5. Payments are not made for each individual shipment; rather, payments are periodically "batched" for each supplier.

ECONOMIC ORDER QUANTITY

Three groups of costs are associated with inventory, as follows:

- **Inventory ordering costs:**
  - Clerical costs
  - Some handling and transportation costs

- **Inventory carrying costs:**
  - Tangible inventory carrying costs:
    - Storage costs.
    - Some handling costs.
    - Property taxes and insurance.
    - Interest on capital invested in inventory.
    - Obsolescence losses.
  - Intangible costs of carrying excessive work-in-process inventory:
    - Erratic production schedules.
    - Inefficient operations.
    - High defect rates.
    - Long lead times.
    - Customer ill will due to erratic performance.
    - Lost sales due to the above problems.

- **Costs of not carrying sufficient inventory:**
  - Customer ill will due to delayed shipments.
  - Expediting orders for products not in stock.
  - Lost sales.

The **economic order quantity** is the order size that results in minimizing the inventory ordering and carrying costs.

THE TABULAR APPROACH TO EOQ

Eakins Company needs 6,000 units of part A105 each year in its production. It costs the company $1.50 per year to carry one of these parts in inventory and it costs $30 to place a purchase order.

Note that if 400 units are ordered at a time the average number of units in inventory during the year will be about 200 units. Inventory will vary from a minimum of zero units just before a new order is received to a maximum of 400 units when the new order arrives. (This assumes zero safety stock, which will be discussed later, and uniform usage throughout the year.)

Symbol*		Order size (units) 300	400	500	600
O/2	Average inventory (units)	150	200	250	300
Q/O	Number of purchase orders	20	15	12	10
C(O/2)	Annual carrying cost	$225	$300	$375	$450
P(Q/O)	Annual purchase order cost	$600	$450	$360	$300
T	Total annual cost	$825	$750	$735	$750

* O = Order size in units.
  Q = Annual quantity used (6,000 in this example).
  C = Annual cost of carrying one unit in stock ($1.50 in this example).
  P = Cost of placing one order ($30 in this example).
  T = Total annual cost.

If the part must be ordered in 100 unit lots, the Economic Order Quantity is 500 units. If the part can be ordered in any quantity, this answer may not be exact.

GRAPHIC APPROACH TO EOQ

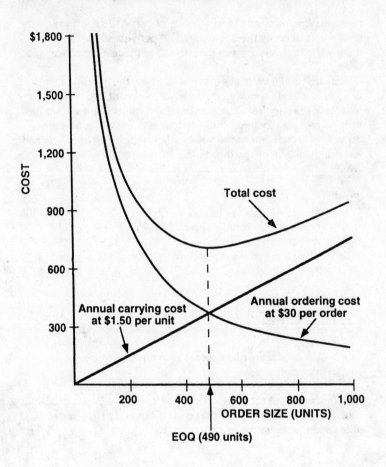

THE FORMULA APPROACH TO EOQ

The economic order quantity (EOQ) can also be found by means of a formula.

$$O = \sqrt{\frac{2QP}{C}}$$

where:

O = Order size in units (EOQ).
Q = Annual quantity used in units.
P = Cost of placing one order.
C = Annual cost of carrying one unit in stock.

Returning to the Eakins Company example, the economic order quantity would be:

$$O = \sqrt{\frac{2(6,000)(\$30)}{\$1.50}}$$

$$O = \sqrt{240,000}$$

$$O = 490 \text{ units}$$

Note that the answer is more exact than that obtained under the tabular approach, since the tabular approach in this particular example dealt only with round 100-unit lots.

REORDER POINT AND SAFETY STOCK

The <u>reorder point</u> tells the manager at what point an item should be reordered. When the inventory of an item drops down to the reorder point, it is time to reorder.

- The reorder point is set so that it is unlikely that the remaining inventory is completely used up before the new order comes in.

- The reorder point depends upon the <u>lead time</u>, the <u>average rate of usage</u>, and the <u>safety stock</u>.

    - The average lead time is the expected delay between when an order is placed with a supplier and when the shipment is received and ready to be used (e.g., 3 weeks).

    - The average rate of usage is the average rate at which the inventory is used up (e.g., 50 units per week are required for production).

    - The product of the average lead time and the average rate of usage is the number of units that are expected to be used up before the new order is received. (For example, 50 units per week X 3 weeks = 150 units.) A manager should never let the inventory slip below this figure since if it does, a stock-out situation is likely to develop before the new order arrives.

REORDER POINT AND SAFETY STOCK (cont'd)

- **The safety stock represents additional stocks that are held in case the order takes longer than expected to fill or the rate of usage is higher than expected.**

- **When the rate of usage is the major uncertainty, the safety stock equals the difference between the maximum expected usage and the average expected usage during the lead time.**

EXAMPLE: Assume the following data for Decker Company:
- Economic Order Quantity . . . . . .   500 units
- Lead time . . . .   3 weeks
- Average expected usage per week . .   50 units
- Maximum expected usage per week .   65 units

Safety stock = (65 units per week - 50 units per week) X 3 weeks
= 45 units

The reorder point is the expected usage of the item during the lead time plus the safety stock:

Reorder point = (Lead time X Average usage) + Safety stock

Reorder point = (3 weeks X 50 units) + 45 units
= 195 units

Thus, the company should place a new order for 500 units (the EOQ) whenever the inventory level drops to 195 units on hand.

SETTING STANDARD COSTS

- A <u>standard</u> can be defined as a benchmark or "norm" for measuring performance.

- The broadest application of the standard cost idea is found in manufacturing firms. Such firms often develop standards in detail for the materials, labor, and overhead cost of each separate product.

IDEAL VS. PRACTICAL STANDARDS

<u>Ideal standards</u> allow for no machine breakdowns or work interruptions, and can be attained only by working at peak effort 100 percent of the time. Such standards:
  - often discourage workers.
  - shouldn't be used for decision making.

<u>Practical standards</u> allow for "normal" machine down time, employee rest periods, and the like. Such standards:
  - are felt to motivate employees, since the standards are "tight but attainable."
  - are useful for decision purposes, since variances from standard will contain only "abnormal" elements.

DIRECT MATERIAL STANDARDS

To illustrate the use of standard costs, consider Speeds, Inc. which manufactures a popular jogging suit. The company wishes to have standard costs developed for the suit in terms of material, labor, and variable overhead.

The <u>standard price per unit</u> for direct materials should be the final, delivered cost of materials. The standard price should reflect:
- Specified quality of materials.
- Quantity discounts.
- Transportation (freight) costs.
- Receiving and handling costs.
- Seasonal availability (if any).

EXAMPLE: A material known as verilon is used in the jogging suits. The standard price for a yard of verilon is determined as follows:

Purchase price, grade A verilon	$5.70
Freight, by truck	.40
Receiving and handling	.10
Less purchase discount in 20,000 yard lots	(.20)
Standard price per yard	$6.00

DIRECT MATERIAL STANDARDS (cont'd)

The <u>standard quantity per unit</u> for direct materials is the amount of material that should go into each finished unit of product. The standard quantity should reflect:
- Engineered (bill of materials) requirements.
- Expected spoilage of raw materials.
- Unavoidable waste of materials in the manufacturing process.
- Materials in scrapped work-in-process (rejects).

EXAMPLE: The standard quantity of verilon that goes into one jogging suit is computed as follows:

Bill of materials requirement	2.8 yds.
Allowance for waste	0.6 yds.
Allowance for rejects	<u>0.1 yds.</u>
Standard quantity per jogging suit	<u>3.5 yds.</u>

Once the price and quantity standards have been set, the <u>standard cost of materials</u> (verilon) for one unit of finished product can be computed:

(3.5 yds./jogging suit) X $6/yd. =$21 per jogging suit

DIRECT LABOR STANDARDS

The <u>standard rate per hour</u> for direct labor
should include all costs associated with direct
labor workers. These costs reflect:
- Hourly wage rates for each worker.
- Expected labor mix (between high and low
  wage rate workers).
- Fringe benefits.
- Employment taxes.

Many companies prepare a single standard rate
for all employees in a department, based on the
expected labor mix. This procedure:
- Simplifies the use of standard costs
- Permits the manager to monitor the mix of
  employees in the department

EXAMPLE: The standard rate per hour for the expected labor mix
is determined by using average wage rates, fringe benefits, and
employment taxes for the labor mix as follows:

Average wage rate per hour $13
Average fringe benefits 4
Average employment taxes 1
Standard rate per direct labor hour $18

DIRECT LABOR STANDARDS (cont'd)

The <u>standard hours per unit</u> for direct labor specifies the amount of direct labor time required to complete one unit of product. This standard time should include:
- Engineered labor time per unit.
- Allowance for breaks, personal needs, and cleanup.
- Allowance for setup and other machine downtime.
- Allowance for rejects.

EXAMPLE: The standard hours required to produce a jogging suit is determined as follows:

Basic labor time per unit	1.4 hrs.
Allowance for breaks and cleanup	0.1 hrs.
Allowance for setup and downtime	0.3 hrs.
Allowance for rejects	<u>0.2</u> hrs.
Standard hours per jogging suit	<u>2.0</u> hrs.

Once the time and rate standards have been set, the <u>standard cost of labor</u> for one unit of product can be computed:

(2.0 hrs./jogging suit) X $18/hr. = $36 per jogging suit.

VARIABLE OVERHEAD STANDARDS

Standards exist for variable overhead, as well as for direct materials and direct labor. The standards are typically expressed in terms of a "rate" and "hours", much like direct labor.

- The "rate" is the variable portion of the predetermined overhead rate.

- The "hours" represent whatever base is used to apply overhead cost to products. Ordinarily, this would be direct labor hours or machine hours.

EXAMPLE: Speeds, Inc. applies overhead cost to products on the basis of direct labor hours. The variable portion of the predetermined overhead rate is $4 per direct labor hour. Using this rate, the standard cost of variable overhead for one unit of product is:

(2.0 hrs./jogging suit) X $4/hr. = $8 per jogging suit.

STANDARD COST CARD

After standards have been set for materials, labor, and overhead, a <u>standard cost card</u> can be prepared. The standard cost card indicates what the final, manufactured cost should be for a unit of product.

EXAMPLE: Referring back to the standard costs computed for materials, labor, and overhead, the standard cost for one jogging suit would be:

<u>Standard Cost Card for Jogging Suits</u>

	(1) Standard Quantity or Hours	(2) Standard Price or Rate	Standard Cost (1) X (2)
Direct Materials	3.5 yds.	$ 6/yd.	$21
Direct labor	2.0 hrs.	18/hr.	36
Variable overhead	2.0 hrs.	4/hr.	8
Total standard cost per suit . .			$65

The data on the standard cost card are used for several purposes, such as:
- Determining the cost of inventories and cost of goods sold.
- Pricing products.
- Control of departmental activities.

THE GENERAL VARIANCE MODEL

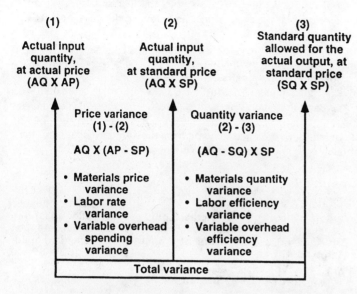

(1)
Actual input
quantity,
at actual price
(AQ X AP)

(2)
Actual input
quantity,
at standard price
(AQ X SP)

(3)
Standard quantity
allowed for the
actual output, at
standard price
(SQ X SP)

Price variance
(1) - (2)

AQ X (AP - SP)

- Materials price
  variance
- Labor rate
  variance
- Variable overhead
  spending
  variance

Quantity variance
(2) - (3)

(AQ - SQ) X SP

- Materials quantity
  variance
- Labor efficiency
  variance
- Variable overhead
  efficiency
  variance

Total variance

The **standard quantity allowed** (**standard hours allowed** in the case of labor and overhead) is the amount of materials, labor, or overhead that should have been used to complete the output of the period.

DIRECT MATERIAL VARIANCES

To illustrate variance analysis, refer to the standard cost card for Speeds, Inc.'s jogging suit. The following data are for last month's production:

Number of suits completed	5,000 units
Cost of material purchased	
(20,000 yds. @ $5.40)	$108,000
Yards of material used	20,000 yds.

Using these data and the data from the standard cost card, the the material price and quantity variances are:

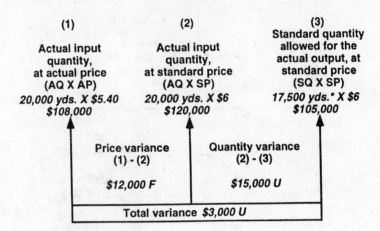

(1)	(2)	(3)
Actual input quantity, at actual price (AQ X AP)	Actual input quantity, at standard price (AQ X SP)	Standard quantity allowed for the actual output, at standard price (SQ X SP)
20,000 yds. X $5.40	20,000 yds. X $6	17,500 yds.* X $6
$108,000	$120,000	$105,000

Price variance
(1) - (2)

$12,000 F

Quantity variance
(2) - (3)

$15,000 U

Total variance $3,000 U

* 5,000 suits X 3.5 yds. per suit = 17,500 yds.
F = Favorable.
U = Unfavorable.

DIRECT MATERIAL VARIANCES (cont'd)

The direct material variances can also be computed as follows:

MATERIAL PRICE VARIANCE:

- **Method one:**
  MPV = (AQ X AP) — (AQ X SP)
      = ($108, 000) — (20,000 yds. X $6.00/yd.) = $12,000 F

- **Method two:**
  MPV = AQ (AP — SP)
      = 20,000 yds. ($5.40/yd. — $6.00/yd.) = $12,000 F

The material price variance should be recorded at the time materials are purchased. This permits:
- **Early recognition of the variance.**
- **Carrying materials in inventory at standard cost.**

MATERIAL QUANTITY VARIANCE:

- **Method one:**
  MQV = (AQ X SP) — (SQ X SP)
        = (20,000 yds. X $6.00/yd.) — (17,500 yds.* X $6.00/yd.)
        = $15,000 U
  *5,000 suits X 3.5 yds. = 17,500 standard yards

- **Method two:**
  MQV = SP (AQ — SQ)
        = $6.00/yd. (20,000 yds. — 17,500 yds.)
        = $15,000 U

DIRECT LABOR VARIANCES

Refer again to the standard cost card for Speeds, Inc.'s jogging suit. The following data are for last month's production:

Number of suits completed (as before) . . . . .   5,000 units
Cost of direct labor (10,500 hrs. @ $20) $210,000

Using these data and the data from the standard cost card, the labor rate and efficiency variances are:

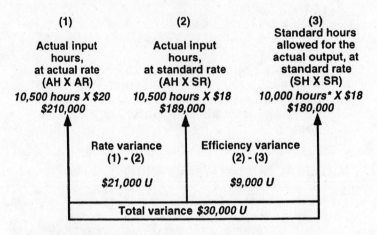

(1)	(2)	(3)
		Standard hours allowed for the
Actual input hours,	**Actual input hours,**	**actual output, at**
at actual rate	**at standard rate**	**standard rate**
(AH X AR)	**(AH X SR)**	**(SH X SR)**
10,500 hours X $20	*10,500 hours X $18*	*10,000 hours* X $18*
$210,000	*$189,000*	*$180,000*

Rate variance
(1) - (2)

$21,000 U

Efficiency variance
(2) - (3)

$9,000 U

Total variance $30,000 U

* 5,000 suits X 2.0 hours per suit = 10,000 hours.
F = Favorable.
U = Unfavorable.

DIRECT LABOR VARIANCES (cont'd)

The direct labor variances can also be computed as follows:

LABOR RATE VARIANCE:

- **Method one:**
  LRV = (AH X AR) — (AH X SR)
    = ($210, 000) — (10,500 hrs. X $18/hr.)
    = $21,000 U

- **Method two:**
  LRV = AH (AR — SR)
    = 10,500 hrs. ($20/hr. — $18/hr.)
    = $21,000 U

LABOR EFFICIENCY VARIANCE:

- **Method one:**
  LEV = (AH X SR) — (SH X SR)
    = (10,500 hrs. X $18/hr.) — (10,000 hrs.* X $18/hr.)
    = $9,000 U
  *5,000 suits X 2..0 hrs. = 10,000 standard hours

- **Method two:**
  LEV = SR (AH — SH)
    = $18/hr. (10,500 hrs. — 10,000 hrs.)
    = $9,000 U

VARIABLE OVERHEAD VARIANCES

Refer again to the standard cost card for Speeds, Inc.'s jogging suit. The following data are for last month's production:

Number of suits completed (as before)	5,000 units
Actual direct labor hours (as before)	10,500 hours
Variable overhead costs incurred	$40,950

Using these data and the data from the standard cost card, the variable overhead variances are:

(1)	(2)	(3)
Actual input hours, at actual rate (AH X AR) (i.e., actual overhead cost)	Actual input hours, at standard rate (AH X SR)	Standard hours allowed for the actual output, at standard rate (SH X SR)
$40,950	10,500 hours X $4 $42,000	10,000 hours* X $4 $40,000

Spending variance (1) - (2)

$1,050 F

Efficiency variance (2) - (3)

$2,000 U

Total variance $950 U

* 5,000 suits X 2.0 hours per suit = 10,000 hours.
  F = Favorable.
  U = Unfavorable.

VARIABLE OVERHEAD VARIANCES (cont'd)

The variable overhead variances can also be computed as follows:

OVERHEAD SPENDING VARIANCE:

- **Method one:**
VOSV = (AH X AR) — (AH X SR)
= ($40,950) — (10,500 hrs. X $4.00/hr.)
= $1,050 F

- **Method two:**
VOSV = AH (AR — SR)
= 10,500 hrs. ($3.90/hr.* — $4.00/hr.)
= $1,050 F
* $40,950 ÷ 10,500 hrs. = $3.90/hr.

OVERHEAD EFFICIENCY VARIANCE:

- **Method one:**
VOEV = (AH X SR) — (SH X SR)
= (10,500 hrs. X $4.00/hr.) — (10,000 hrs.** X $4.00/hr.)
= $2,000 U
**5,000 suits X 2.0 hrs. = 10,000 standard hours

- **Method two:**
VOEV = SR (AH — SH)
= $4.00/hr. (10,500 hrs. — 10,000 hrs.)
= $2,000 U

JOURNAL ENTRIES FOR VARIANCES

Materials, work-in-process, and finished goods are all carried in inventory at their respective standard costs in a standard costing system.

Purchase of materials:

Raw materials (20,000 yards at $6.00)	120,000	
Materials price variance (20,000 yards at $0.60 F)		12,000
Accounts payable (20,000 yards at $5.40)		108,000

Use of materials:

Work-in-process (17,500 yards at $6)	105,000	
Materials quantity variance (2,500 yards U at $6)	15,000	
Raw materials (20,000 yards at $6)		120,000

Direct labor cost:

Work-in-process (10,000 hours at $18)	180,000	
Labor rate variance (10,500 hours at $2 U)	21,000	
Labor efficiency variance (500 hours U at $18)	9,000	
Wages payable (10,500 hours at $20)		210,000

PERFORMANCE MEASURES IN THE NEW COMPETITIVE ENVIRONMENT

SHORTCOMINGS OF STANDARD COSTS

- Standard cost variances are often reported to managers too late for them to take timely corrective action.

- Labor has become less significant and tends to be more fixed. A focus on labor efficiency variances tends to encourage production of excess inventories.

- A key objective in the new manufacturing environment is to increase quality. An overemphasis on cost may result in lower quality. For example, focussing on the materials price variance may result in the purchase of low quality materials.

- Competitive conditions often require continuous improvement; attaining preset standards isn't sufficient.

- The manufacturing process is more reliable and consistent in an automated environment and as a result the traditional variances are either minimal or cease to exist.

PERFORMANCE MEASURES IN THE NEW COMPETITIVE ENVIRONMENT (cont'd)

THE NEW PERFORMANCE MEASURES

- Many are nonfinancial, emphasizing key operational measures such as the percentage of on-time deliveries.

- The new performance measures are often computed "on-line" on a "real-time" basis so that managers and workers are able to monitor operations continually and take corrective actions immediately.

- Some measures are computed at the plant level in order to emphasize the importance of integrated, interdependent operation.

- Managers focus on trends over time. The key objectives are progress and improvement, rather than meeting any specific preset standards.

OPERATING MEASURES IN A JIT / FMS SETTING

	Desired Change
Quality Control Measures	
Number of warranty claims	Decrease
Number of customer complaints	Decrease
Number of defects	Decrease
First-time pass rate	Increase
Field failure rate	Decrease
Total quality cost	Decrease
Material Control Measures	
Material as a percentage of total cost	Decrease
Lead time	Decrease
Scrap as a percentage of good pieces	Decrease
Scrap as a percentage of total cost	Decrease
Actual scrap loss	Decrease
Inventory Control Measures	
Inventory turnover:	
Raw materials (by type)	Increase
Finished goods (by product)	Increase
Number of inventoried items	Decrease
Machine Performance Measures	
Percentage of machine availability	Increase
Percentage of machine downtime	Decrease
Use as a percentage of availability	Increase
Setup time	Decrease
Delivery Performance Measures	
Percentage of on-time deliveries	Increase
Delivery cycle-time	Decrease
Throughput time, or velocity	Decrease
Manufacturing cycle efficiency (MCE)	Increase
Order backlog	Decrease
Total throughput, or output rate	Increase

DELIVERY CYCLE TIME AND THROUGHPUT TIME

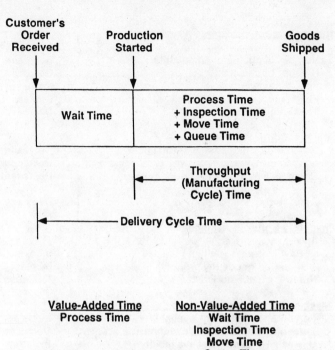

DELIVERY PERFORMANCE MEASURES

The purpose of production is to get high-quality products into the hands of customers as quickly as possible. There are several key measures of delivery performance:
- Percentage of on-time deliveries.
- Delivery cycle time.
- Throughput time (also known as manufacturing cycle time or the velocity of production).

• Throughput time can be put into better perspective by computing the manufacturing cycle efficiency (MCE). MCE is defined by:

$$MCE = \frac{Value\text{--}added\ time}{Throughput\ time}$$

If the MCE is less than 1, "non-value-added" time is present in the production process.

An MCE of 0.4 would mean that 60% (1.0 - 0.4 = 0.6) of the total production time consists of waiting, inspection, and move time, and therefore only 40% of the total time is productive.

By monitoring and improving MCE, companies are able to pare away "non-value-added" activities.

STATIC BUDGETS

The budgets in the previous chapter were "static." A <u>static budget</u> is valid for only one level of activity such as the planned level of activity. Sometimes firms compare actual results to the static budget, but such a comparison has limited usefulness.

EXAMPLE: Scott Company, which makes a single product, bases its annual budget on the following data:

Budgeted output	10,000 units

Variable cost category	Standard cost _per unit_
Maintenance	$ 0.60
Indirect materials	1.40
Utilities	1.00
Total variable cost	$3.00

Fixed cost category	Budgeted _annual cost_
Depreciation	$ 40,000
Supervision	50,000
Insurance	10,000
Total fixed cost	$100,000

STATIC BUDGETS (cont'd)

Even though Scott Company had budgeted to produce and sell
10,000 units during the year, actual activity was only 8,000 units.
A report based upon the static (i.e., original) budget from the
beginning of the year follows.

Scott Company
Comparison of Actual Spending to the Budgeted Spending

	Actual	Original Budget	Variance	
Units produced and sold .	8,000	10,000	2,000	U
Variable overhead costs:				
Maintenance	$ 4,500	$ 6,000	$ 1,500	F
Indirect materials	12,000	14,000	2,000	F
Utilities	9,500	10,000	500	F
Total variable costs	26,000	30,000	4,000	F
Fixed overhead costs:				
Depreciation	40,000	40,000	—	
Supervision	49,000	50,000	1,000	F
Insurance	10,000	10,000	—	
Total fixed overhead . . .	99,000	100,000	1,000	F
Total overhead costs . . .	$125,000	$130,000	$5,000	F

Does the above report, which is based on the original static
budget, reliably indicate whether overhead spending was under
control?

FLEXIBLE BUDGETS

A <u>flexible budget</u> differs considerably from a static budget.
- A flexible budget is geared toward all levels of activity within the relevant range, rather than toward only one level of activity.
- A flexible budget is dynamic rather than static; it can be tailored for any level of activity within the relevant range.

EXAMPLE: Refer to the data for Scott Company. A flexible budget for overhead is provided below for three different levels of activity ranging from 5,000 to 15,000 units.

Scott Company
Flexible Budget for Overhead

	Cost per unit	Units 5,000	Units 10,000	Units 15,000
Variable overhead costs:				
Maintenance	$0.60	$ 3,000	$ 6,000	$ 9,000
Indirect materials . .	1.40	7,000	14,000	21,000
Utilities	1.00	5,000	10,000	15,000
Total variable costs. .	$3.00	15,000	30,000	45,000
Fixed overhead costs:				
Depreciation		40,000	40,000	40,000
Supervision		50,000	50,000	50,000
Insurance		10,000	10,000	10,000
Total fixed overhead .		100,000	100,000	100,000
Total overhead costs .		$115,000	$130,000	$145,000

OVERHEAD PERFORMANCE REPORT

When the actual level of activity differs from what had been assumed in the budget from the beginning of the period, we would expect spending to differ as well. In a performance report, actual costs are compared to the flexible budget for the actual level of activity.

EXAMPLE: Since Scott Company produced and sold only 8,000 units instead of the 10,000 units that had been planned, we would expect spending on variable overhead items to be less than had been planned.

Scott Company
Overhead Performance Report

	Cost per unit	Actual 8,000 Units	Budget 8,000 Units	Spending & Budget Variances
Variable overhead costs:				
Maintenance	$0.60	$ 4,500	$ 4,800	$ 300 F
Indirect materials . .	1.40	12,000	11,200	800 U
Utilities	1.00	9,500	8,000	1,500 U
Total variable costs. . .	$3.00	26,000	24,000	2,000 U
Fixed overhead costs:				
Depreciation		40,000	40,000	—
Supervision		49,000	50,000	1,000 F
Insurance		10,000	10,000	—
Total fixed overhead .		99,000	100,000	1,000 F
Total overhead costs .		$125,000	$124,000	$1,000 U

Note the contrast between this performance report and the report based upon the static budget.

THE MEASURE OF ACTIVITY

• Most companies use a measure of inputs such as labor or machine hours as an activity base instead of units. This is particularly true in multi-product firms where hours can serve as a common denominator across diverse products.

• Should actual hours or standard hours allowed for the actual output be used in constructing budget allowances for the performance report? There are two approaches:

1. The budget allowance is based solely on the actual hours. Then only a spending variance is computed. (See Exhibit 11-6 in the text for an example.)

2. Budget allowances are based on both the actual hours and the standard hours allowed for the actual output. Then both spending and efficiency variances are computed. (See Exhibit 11-7 in the text for an example.)

VARIABLE OVERHEAD PERFORMANCE REPORT:
BUDGET ALLOWANCES BASED ON ACTUAL HOURS
(Exhibit 11-6)

DONNER COMPANY

Variable Overhead Performance Report
For the Year Ended March 31, 19x1

Budget allowances are based on 42,000 machine-hours actually worked.

Comparing the budget against actual overhead cost yields only a spending variance.

Budgeted machine-hours 50,000
Actual machine-hours 42,000
Standard machine-hours allowed 40,000

Overhead Costs	Cost Formula (per hour)	Actual Costs Incurred 42,000 Hours	Budget Based on 42,000 Hours	Spending Variance	
Variable costs:					
Indirect labor	$0.80	$36,000	$33,600*	$2,400	U
Lubricants	0.30	11,000	12,600	1,600	F
Power.	0.40	24,000	16,800	7,200	U
Total variable costs.	$1.50	$71,000	$63,000	$8,000	U

* 42,000 hours × $0.80 = $33,600. Other budget allowances are computed in the same way.

BUDGET ALLOWANCES BASED ON ACTUAL HOURS
AND STANDARD HOURS ALLOWED
(Exhibit 11-7)

DONNER COMPANY

Variable Overhead Performance Report
For the Year Ended March 31, 19x1

Budget allowances are based on 40,000 machine-hours—the time it *should have taken* to produce 20,000 units of output—as well as on the 42,000 *actual* machine-hours worked.

This approach yields both a spending and an efficiency variance.

Budgeted machine-hours 50,000
Actual machine-hours 42,000
Standard machine-hours allowed 40,000

Overhead Costs	Cost Formula (per hour)	(1) Actual Costs Incurred 42,000 Hours	(2) Budget Based on 42,000 Hours	(3) Budget Based on 40,000 Hours	(4) Total Variance (1) – (3)		Spending Variance (1) – (2)		Efficiency Variance (2) – (3)	
Variable costs:										
Indirect labor	$0.80	$36,000	$33,600*	$32,000	$ 4,000	U	$2,400	U	$1,600	U
Lubricants	0.30	11,000	12,600	12,000	1,000	F	1,600	F	600	U
Power	0.40	24,000	16,800	16,000	8,000	U	7,200	U	800	U
Total variable costs	$1.50	$71,000	$63,000	$60,000	$11,000	U	$8,000	U	$3,000	U

The last two columns appear under the heading "Breakdown of the Total Variance".

* 42,000 hours × $0.80 = $33,600. Other budget allowances are computed in the same way.

©Richard D. Irwin, Inc., 1994

OVERHEAD VARIANCE ANALYSIS

The flexible budget provides information to:
- Compute predetermined overhead rates.
- Complete the standard cost card.
- Apply overhead cost to products.
- Prepare overhead variance reports.

EXAMPLE: Swift Company manufactures a single product.
Standard cost data for the product follows:

	Standard Quantity or Hours	Standard Price or Rate	Standard Cost (1) X (2)
Direct Materials . . .	3.5 feet	$12/foot	$42
Direct labor	2.0 hours	$16/hour	$32

Overhead is assigned to the product on the basis of standard direct labor hours. Swift Company's flexible budget for overhead (in condensed form) is given below:

	Cost Per DLH	Direct Labor Hours		
		10,000	15,000	20,000
Variable costs	$5	$ 50,000	$ 75,000	$100,000
Fixed costs		300,000	300,000	300,000
Total overhead costs .		$350,000	$375,000	$400,000

PREDETERMINED OVERHEAD RATES

The predetermined overhead rate used to cost units of product depends on the <u>denominator activity</u> level.

EXAMPLE: The predetermined overhead rate at Swift Company is computed below for two levels of activity: 10,000 DLH and 15,000 DLH.

	Denominator activity
10,000 DLH	_15,000 DLH_

Variable element of the predetermined overhead rate:

$$\frac{\$50,000}{10,000 \text{ DLH}} = \$5 / \text{DLH} \qquad \frac{\$75,000}{15,000 \text{ DLH}} = \$5 / \text{DLH}$$

Fixed element of the predetermined overhead rate:

$$\frac{\$300,000}{10,000 \text{ DLH}} = \$30 / \text{DLH} \qquad \frac{\$300,000}{15,000 \text{ DLH}} = \$20 / \text{DLH}$$

Predetermined overhead rate:

$$\frac{\$350,000}{10,000 \text{ DLH}} = \$35 / \text{DLH} \qquad \frac{\$375,000}{15,000 \text{ DLH}} = \$25 / \text{DLH}$$

Note that the difference between the predetermined overhead rates at the two levels of denominator activity is entirely due to fixed overhead.

OVERHEAD COST APPLICATION
IN A STANDARD COST SYSTEM

Assume that 15,000 DLH is used as the denominator level of activity. The following data apply to the current year's operations.

Denominator activity level	15,000 DLH
Number of units completed	8,000 units
Actual direct labor hours	18,000 DLH
Actual overhead cost incurred:	
Variable	$ 81,000
Fixed	305,000
Total	$386,000

In a standard cost system, overhead is applied on the basis of the standard hours allowed for the actual output rather than on the basis of the actual hours. This results in a simpler system in which the overhead applied to a unit is always the same. In this example, the overhead cost per unit is always $50 (2.0 hours X $25 per hour).

Using the above data, the company's manufacturing overhead account would appear as follows:

	Manufacturing Overhead	
Actual overhead costs	386,000	400,000 * Applied overhead costs
		14,000 Overapplied overhead cost

* 8,000 units x 2.0 hrs./unit = 16,000 hrs.;
  16,000 hrs. x $25/hr. = $400,000.

VARIABLE OVERHEAD VARIANCES

Swift Company's $14,000 overapplied overhead can be explained by four variances: the variable overhead spending and efficiency variances and the fixed overhead budget and volume variances. The variable overhead variances are computed below:

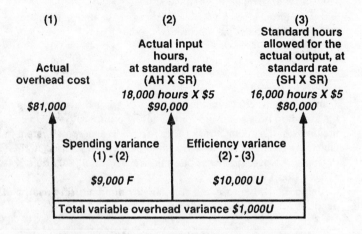

(1)	(2)	(3)
		Standard hours allowed for the
	Actual input hours,	actual output, at
Actual	at standard rate	standard rate
overhead cost	(AH X SR)	(SH X SR)
	18,000 hours X $5	*16,000 hours X $5*
$81,000	*$90,000*	*$80,000*

Spending variance
(1) - (2)

$9,000 F

Efficiency variance
(2) - (3)

$10,000 U

Total variable overhead variance *$1,000U*

<u>Spending variance:</u> The variable overhead spending variance contains elements of waste or excessive usage as well as differences between actual and standard prices.

<u>Efficiency variance:</u> The variable overhead efficiency variance is <u>not</u> a measure of the efficiency of overhead. It is a measure of the efficiency in the <u>base</u> underlying the flexible budget—in this case, direct labor.

FIXED OVERHEAD VARIANCES

Relevant data concerning Swift Company are presented below:

Denominator activity (direct labor hours)	15,000 DLH
Actual direct labor hours worked	18,000 DLH
Standard direct labor hours allowed for output . .	16,000 DLH
Number of units produced	8,000 units
Flexible budget fixed overhead cost	$300,000
Actual fixed overhead cost incurred	$305,000
Fixed element of the predetermined overhead rate	$20

Using these data, an analysis of the company's fixed overhead variances follows:

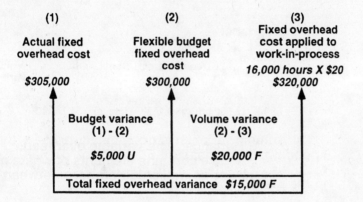

(1)	(2)	(3)
Actual fixed overhead cost	**Flexible budget fixed overhead cost**	**Fixed overhead cost applied to work-in-process**
		16,000 hours X $20
$305,000	*$300,000*	*$320,000*

Budget variance (1) - (2) — *$5,000 U*

Volume variance (2) - (3) — *$20,000 F*

Total fixed overhead variance *$15,000 F*

FIXED OVERHEAD VARIANCES (cont'd)

The fixed overhead variances can also be computed as follows:

Budget Variance:

Actual fixed overhead cost	$305,000
Flexible budget fixed overhead cost	300,000
Budget variance	$ 5,000 U

The budget variance is similar to the variable overhead spending variance.

Volume Variance:

$$\text{Fixed portion of the predetermined overhead rate} \times \left(\text{Denominator hours} - \text{Standard hours allowed} \right) = \text{Volume Variance}$$

$$\$20 \times (15{,}000 \text{ hours} - 16{,}000 \text{ hours}) = \$20{,}000 \text{ F}$$

The volume variance is not a measure of spending; it is a measure of utilization of plant facilities. It is affected only by the level of activity in the plant.

SUMMARY OF VARIANCES

To summarize, the cause of under- or over-applied overhead can be explained in terms of:

- **Variable overhead**

  - **Variable overhead spending variance**

  - **Variable overhead efficiency variance (when overhead is applied on the basis of standard hours)**

- **Fixed overhead**

  - **Fixed overhead budget variance**

  - **Fixed overhead volume variance**

Thus, the cause of Swift Company's $14,000 overapplied overhead can be explained by:

Variable overhead:	
Spending variance	$ 9,000 F
Efficiency variance	10,000 U
Fixed overhead:	
Budget variance	5,000 U
Volume variance	20,000 F
Overapplied overhead	$14,000 F

These variances would appear on Swift Company's income statement as an adjustment to Cost of Goods Sold.

GRAPHIC ANALYSIS
OF VOLUME VARIANCE

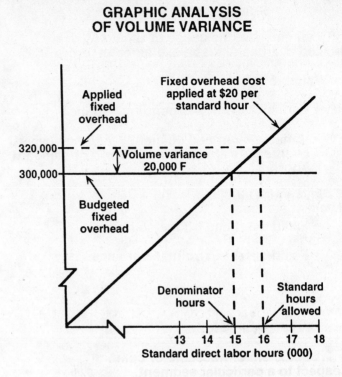

SEGMENTED REPORTING

To operate effectively, managers need more than a single, company-wide income statement; they need statements that focus on the various segments of a company.

DEFINITION OF A SEGMENT

A <u>segment</u> is any part or activity of an organization about which a manager seeks cost or revenue data. Examples of segments include: sales territories, products, divisions of a company, individual salespersons, etc.

Segmented statements can be prepared at many levels of a company.

ALLOCATION GUIDELINES

Two guidelines should be followed in assigning costs to the various segments of a company:
1. First, according to cost behavior patterns.
2. Second, according to whether the costs are directly traceable to the segments involved.

TRACEABLE AND COMMON COSTS

A cost is either traceable or common with respect to a particular segment.

<u>Traceable costs</u> arise because of the existence of the particular segment.

<u>Common costs</u> arise because of overall operating activities and are not due to the existence of a particular segment.

SEGMENT REPORTING EXAMPLE

	Total Company	Division A	Division B
Sales	$1,500,000	$900,000	$600,000
Less variable costs	800,000	450,000	350,000
Contribution margin	700,000	450,000	250,000
Less traceable fixed costs	400,000	230,000	170,000*
Divisional segment margin	300,000	$220,000	$ 80,000
Less common fixed costs	240,000		
Net income	$ 60,000		

	Division B	Product Line 1	Product Line 2
Sales	$600,000	$400,000	$200,000
Less variable costs	350,000	200,000	150,000
Contribution margin	250,000	200,000	50,000
Less traceable fixed costs	100,000	40,000	60,000
Product line segment margin	150,000	$160,000	$(10,000)
Less common fixed costs	70,000		
Divisional segment margin	$ 80,000		

*The $170,000 in traceable fixed expenses for Division B changes to $100,000 traceable and $70,000 common when Division B is segmented by product lines.

GRAPHIC PRESENTATION OF SEGMENT REPORTING
(Exhibit 12-4)

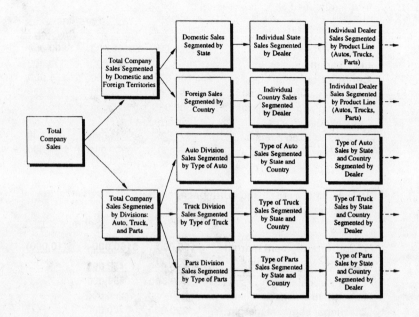

DANGERS IN ALLOCATING COMMON COSTS

Common costs should <u>not</u> be allocated among segments. If common costs are allocated, then the results can be misleading to management.

EXAMPLE: Suppose that in the segment reporting example the company had allocated common costs on the basis of sales (a frequently used allocation basis).

	Total Company	Division A	Division B
Sales	$1,500,000	$900,000	$600,000
Less variable costs	800,000	450,000	350,000
Contribution margin	700,000	450,000	250,000
Less traceable fixed costs	400,000	230,000	170,000
Divisional segment margin	300,000	220,000	80,000
Less allocated common fixed costs	240,000	144,000	96,000
Net income	$ 60,000	$ 76,000	$(16,000)

If Division B were closed down because of its apparent loss, the following would occur:

	Total Company	Division A	Division B
Sales	$900,000	$900,000	—
Less variable costs	450,000	450,000	—
Contribution margin	450,000	450,000	—
Less traceable fixed costs	230,000	230,000	—
Divisional segment margin	220,000	220,000	—
Less allocated common fixed costs	240,000	240,000	—
Net income	$(20,000)	$(20,000)	—

©Richard D. Irwin, Inc., 1994

SEGMENTS CLASSIFIED AS COST, PROFIT, AND INVESTMENT CENTERS
(Exhibit 12-5)

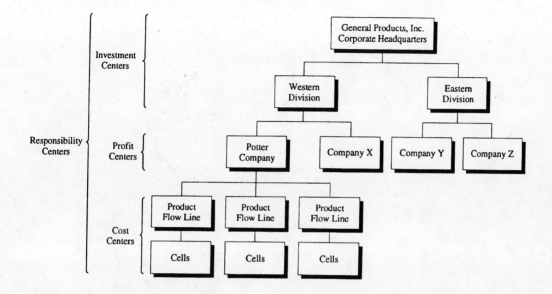

RETURN ON INVESTMENT

The return on investment (ROI) formula is:

Margin X Turnover = ROI

or, in detailed form:

$$\frac{\text{Net operating income}}{\text{Sales}} \times \frac{\text{Sales}}{\text{Average operating assets}} = ROI$$

EXAMPLE: Regal Company reports the following data:

Net operating income $30,000
Sales $500,000
Average operating assets $200,000

$$\frac{\$30,000}{\$500,000} \times \frac{\$500,000}{\$200,000} = ROI$$

6%   X   2.5   = 15%

There are three ways in which a manager can improve ROI:
1. Increase sales.
2. Reduce expenses.
3. Reduce operating assets.

RETURN ON INVESTMENT (cont'd)

Approach 1—Increase sales:

Assume that Regal Company is able to increase sales to $600,000. Net operating income increases to $42,000, and the operating assets remain unchanged.

$$\frac{\$42,000}{\$600,000} \times \frac{\$600,000}{\$200,000} = ROI$$

$$7\% \quad X \quad 3.0 \quad = 21\%$$

(as compared to 15% before)

Approach 2—Reduce expenses:

Assume that Regal Company is able to reduce expenses by $10,000 per year, so that net operating income increases from $30,000 to $40,000. Sales and operating assets remain unchanged.

$$\frac{\$40,000}{\$500,000} \times \frac{\$500,000}{\$200,000} = ROI$$

$$8\% \quad X \quad 2.5 \quad = 20\%$$

(as compared to 15% before)

Approach 3—Reduce assets:

Assume that Regal Company is able to reduce its average operating assets from $200,000 to $125,000. Sales and net operating income remain unchanged.

$$\frac{\$30,000}{\$500,000} \times \frac{\$500,000}{\$125,000} = ROI$$

$$6\% \quad X \quad 4.0 \quad = 24\%$$

(as compared to 15% before)

RESIDUAL INCOME

Residual income is the net operating income that an investment center is able to earn above the minimum rate of return on its operating assets.

EXAMPLE: Marsh Company has two divisions, A and B. Division A has $1,000,000 in operating assets and Division B has $3,000,000 in operating assets. Each division is required to earn a minimum return of 12% on its investment in operating assets.

	Division A	Division B
Average operating assets	$1,000,000	$3,000,000
Net operating income last year . .	$ 200,000	$ 450,000
Minimum required return:		
12% X average operating assets	120,000	360,000
Residual income	$ 80,000	$ 90,000

A disadvantage of the residual income approach is that it can't readily be used to compare the performance of divisions of different sizes.

RESIDUAL INCOME (cont'd)

Some companies believe residual income is a better measure of performance than ROI. The residual income approach encourages managers to make profitable investments that would be rejected under the ROI approach.

EXAMPLE: Marsh Company's Division A has an opportunity to make an investment of $250,000 that would generate a return of 16% on invested assets (i.e., $40,000 per year). This investment would be in the best interests of the company since the rate of return of 16% exceeds the minimum required rate of return.

However, this investment would reduce the division's ROI:

	Present	New Project	Overall
Average operating assets (a)	$1,000,000	$250,000	$1,250,000
Net operating income (b) . .	$200,000	$40,000	$240,000
ROI (b) ÷ (a)	20.0%	16.0%	19.2%

On the other hand, this investment would increase the division's residual income:

	Present	New Project	Overall
Average operating assets .	$1,000,000	$250,000	$1,250,000
Net operating income . . .	$200,000	$40,000	$240,000
Minimum required return:			
12% X Ave. operating assets	120,000	30,000	150,000
Residual income	$ 80,000	$10,000	$ 90,000

TRANSFER PRICING

A <u>transfer price</u> is the price charged when one segment (for example, a division) provides goods or services to another segment of the same company.

- Transfer prices are necessary to calculate costs in a cost, profit, or investment center.

- One party to the transaction will naturally want a low transfer price and the other will want a high transfer price.

- From the standpoint of the firm as a whole, transfer prices involve "taking money out of one pocket and putting it into the other."

- An <u>optimal transfer price</u> is one that leads division managers to make decisions that are in the best interests of the firm as a whole.

In practice three general approaches are used in setting transfer prices:

1. Cost-based price.
   a. Variable cost.
   b. Full (absorption) cost.

2. Market price.

3. Negotiated price.

COST-BASED TRANSFER PRICES

Transfer prices based on cost are common; probably because they are easily understood and convenient to use. Unfortunately, cost-based transfer prices have several disadvantages:

- Cost-based transfer prices can lead to bad decisions. (For example, they don't include opportunity costs from lost sales.)

- The only division that will show any profits is the one that makes the final sale to an outside party.

- Cost-based transfer prices provide no incentive for control of costs unless transfers are made at standard cost.

MARKET-BASED TRANSFER PRICES

Some form of competitive market price is widely regarded as the best practical approach to transfer pricing. When there is an active market for the intermediate good or service, the market price will often be a suitable transfer price — particularly when there is no idle capacity in the transferring division.

NEGOTIATED TRANSFER PRICES

When division managers can work well together, a negotiated transfer price is an excellent solution to the transfer pricing problem. If a transfer is in the best interests of the entire company, division managers bargaining in good faith should be able to find a compromise transfer price that makes all of the divisions better off.

The transfer price is a means of "cutting up the pie" of company profits among the divisions. If the entire pie is bigger because of a transfer, it is always possible to cut the pie in such a way that each piece is also bigger.

OPTIMAL TRANSFER PRICES

In general, to arrive at an optimal transfer price:

1. Decide whether it is in the best interests of the entire firm for the transfer to take place.

2. Select a transfer price (or range of transfer prices) that should motivate the managers to do what is in the best interests of the firm.

Often, there will be no single optimal transfer price. Instead, there will be a range of transfer prices that should induce the optimal behavior. Some sort of rule or negotiations can be used to arrive at the exact transfer price that will be used.

OPTIMAL TRANSFER PRICES

EXAMPLE: The Battery Division of Barker Company makes a standard 12-volt battery.

Production capacity (number of batteries) 300,000
Selling price per battery to outsiders $40
Variable costs per battery $18
Fixed costs per battery (based on capacity) $7

Barker Company has a Vehicle Division that could use this battery in its forklift trucks. The Vehicle Division is now buying 100,000 batteries per year from an outside supplier at $39 per battery.

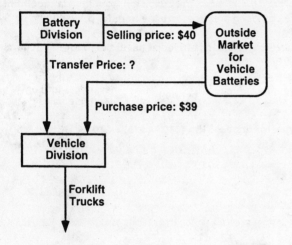

OPTIMAL TRANSFER PRICES (cont'd)

Situation 1:

Suppose the Battery Division is operating at capacity. What price per battery should be charged to the Vehicle Division?

If a battery is transferred from the Battery Division to the Vehicle Division, the firm (and the Battery Division) will lose revenues of $40. Since suitable batteries can be purchased from an outside supplier for only $39, no transfers should be made.

The cost to the firm and to the Battery Division of a transfer is $40 in lost revenue. If the transfer price is set at $40, the Vehicle Division manager will purchase batteries from the outside supplier. This is the correct decision from the standpoint of the whole company and therefore the transfer price should be $40.

This answer can be arrived at using the following general formula:

$$\text{Transfer price} = \frac{\text{Variable costs}}{\text{per unit}} + \frac{\text{Lost contribution}}{\text{margin per unit on outside sales}}$$

Transfer price = $18 + ($40 — $18) = $40

OPTIMAL TRANSFER PRICES (cont'd)

Situation 2:

Assume again that the Battery Division is operating at capacity, but suppose that the division can avoid $4 in variable costs, such as selling commissions, on intracompany sales. What price per battery should be charged to the Vehicle Division?

If a battery is transferred from the Battery Division to the Vehicle Division in this situation, the firm (and the Battery Division) will lose revenues of $40, but will save $4 in variable costs. Therefore, the net cost of the transfer from the viewpoint of the company as a whole is $36. Since this is less than the cost of purchasing batteries from an outside supplier, the batteries should be acquired from the Battery Division.

The Battery Division will be fully compensated for its lost sales if the transfer price is at least $36. The Vehicle Division manager will make the correct decision from the standpoint of the company as a whole if the transfer price is less than $39. Therefore, the optimal transfer price should be between $36 and $39.

$$\$36 \leq \text{Optimal Transfer Price} \leq \$39$$

The formula approach provides the <u>lower limit</u> for the optimal transfer price:

$$\text{Transfer price} = \frac{\text{Variable costs}}{\text{per unit}} + \frac{\text{Lost contribution}}{\text{margin per unit on}}_{\text{outside sales}}$$

Transfer price = ($18 - $4) + ($40 — $18) = $14 + $12 = $36

OPTIMAL TRANSFER PRICES (cont'd)

Situation 3:

Refer to the original data. Assume that the Battery Division has enough idle capacity to supply the Vehicle Division's needs without diverting batteries from the outside market. What price per battery should be charged to the Vehicle Division?

In this situation if the batteries are transferred to the Vehicle Division, there are no lost sales. On the other hand, variable costs of $18 would be incurred to make each additional battery. (In this situation the batteries would not have been made anyway.) Therefore, the cost to the company (and to the Battery Division) would be $18 per battery. Since this is less than the cost of acquiring batteries on the outside market, the transfers should be made.

The Battery Division will be fully compensated for its costs if the transfer price is at least $18. The Vehicle Division manager will make the correct decision from the standpoint of the company as a whole if the transfer price is less than $39. Therefore, the optimal transfer price should be somewhere between $18 and $39.

$$\$18 \leq \text{Optimal Transfer Price} \leq \$39$$

Again, the formula approach provides the <u>lower limit</u> for the optimal transfer price:

$$\text{Transfer price} = \frac{\text{Variable costs}}{\text{per unit}} + \frac{\text{Lost contribution}}{\text{margin per unit on}}_{\text{outside sales}}$$

Transfer price = $18 + $0 = $18

OPTIMAL TRANSFER PRICES (cont'd)

Situation 4:

The Vehicle Division wants the Battery Division to supply it with 50,000 special heavy duty batteries.

- The variable cost for each heavy duty battery would be $27.
- The Battery Division has no idle capacity.
- Heavy duty batteries require more processing time than regular batteries; they would displace 75,000 regular batteries from the production line.

Selling price, regular battery	$40
Variable costs, regular battery	-$18
Contribution margin, regular battery	$22
Unit sales lost	X 75,000
Contribution margin lost	$1,650,000
Unit sales, heavy duty battery	+ 50,000
Lost contribution margin per heavy duty battery	$33

Since each heavy duty battery costs the company $27 in variable costs and $33 in lost contribution margin, the transfer price should be $60. In this situation we don't know the Vehicle Division's other alternatives, but a transfer price of $60 will send the right "signal" to the Vehicle Division's manager concerning the cost to the company of making the heavy duty batteries.

The formula approach yields the same answer:

$$\text{Transfer price} = \frac{\text{Variable costs}}{\text{per unit}} + \frac{\text{Lost contribution}}{\text{margin per unit on outside sales}}$$

Transfer price = $27 + $33 = $60

TRANSFER PRICING EXERCISES

	Case 1	Case 2	Case 3	Case 4
Division A capacity	100,000	500,000	250,000	400,000
Division A outside sales	100,000	500,000	200,000	300,000
Division B needs	30,000	80,000	50,000	100,000
Division A:				
Normal variable cost	$40	$ 60	$30	$50
Variable costs avoided on internal sales	—	$10	—	$2
Fixed cost per unit based on capacity	$10	$25	$8	$12
Outside selling price	$70	$100	$45	$80
Division B:				
Purchase price from outside supplier	$68	$96	$43	$75
Optimal range of transfer prices	?	?	?	?

Answers:
Case 1: $70
Case 2, $90 ≤ optimal transfer price ≤ $96
Case 3, $30 ≤ optimal transfer price ≤ $43
Case 4, $48 ≤ optimal transfer price ≤ $75.

RELEVANT COSTS

A <u>relevant cost</u> is a cost that is avoidable as a result of choosing one alternative over another.

All costs are considered to be avoidable, except:
- Sunk costs.
- Future costs that do not differ between the alternatives at hand.

A relevant cost can also be defined as any cost (or revenue) that differs between the alternatives being considered.

HOW TO IDENTIFY RELEVANT COSTS

A manager should follow the steps below in identifying the costs (and revenues) that are relevant in a decision:

1. Assemble all of the costs and revenues associated with each alternative.

2. Eliminate those costs that are sunk.

3. Eliminate those costs and revenues that do not differ between alternatives.

4. Make a decision based on the remaining costs and revenues. These are the costs and revenues that are differential or avoidable, and hence relevant to the decision to be made.

RELEVANT COST EXAMPLE

EXAMPLE: White Company is considering replacing an old machine with a new, more efficient machine. Data on the machines follow:

New machine:
List price new	$90,000
Annual variable expenses	$80,000
Expected life	5 years

Old machine:
Original cost	$72,000
Remaining book value	$60,000
Disposal value now	$15,000
Annual variable expenses	$100,000
Remaining life	5 years

White Company's sales are $200,000 per year and fixed expenses (other than depreciation) are $70,000 per year. Should the new machine be purchased?

Incorrect solution:

Some managers would not purchase the new machine since disposal of the old machine would apparently result in a loss:

Remaining book value	$60,000
Disposal value now	15,000
Loss from disposal	$45,000

RELEVANT COST EXAMPLE (cont'd)

<u>Correct solution:</u>

The remaining book value of the old machine is a sunk cost that can't be avoided by the company. This can be shown by looking at comparative cost and revenue data for the next five years taken together:

	5 Years Together		
	Keep Old Machine	Purchase New Machine	Differential Costs
Sales	$1,000,000	$1,000,000	$ —
Variable expenses	(500,000)	(400,000)	100,000
Other fixed expenses	(350,000)	(350,000)	—
Depreciation of the new machine	—	(90,000)	(90,000)
Depreciation of the old machine, or book value write-off	(60,000)	(60,000)	—
Disposal value of the old machine	—	15,000	15,000
Total net income.	$ 90,000	$ 115,000	$ 25,000

Using only relevant costs, the solution would be:

Savings in variable expenses provided by the new machine ($20,000* X 5 yrs.)	$100,000
Cost of the new machine	(90,000)
Disposal value of the old machine	15,000
Net advantage of the new machine	$ 25,000

* $100,000 — $80,000 = $20,000.

DROP OR RETAIN A SEGMENT

One of the most frequently used applications involving relevant costs is in decisions concerning whether a segment such as a product line should be retained or dropped.

EXAMPLE: Due to the declining popularity of digital watches, Sweiz Company's digital watch line has not reported a profit for several years. An income statement for last year follows:

Segment Income Statement— Digital Watches

Sales		$ 500,000
Less variable expenses:		
Variable manufacturing costs	$120,000	
Variable shipping costs	5,000	
Commissions	75,000	200,000
Contribution margin		300,000
Less fixed expenses:		
General factory overhead *	60,000	
Salary of line manager	90,000	
Depreciation of equipment* *	50,000	
Advertising—direct	100,000	
Rent—factory space	70,000	
General administrative expense* . . .	30,000	400,000
Net loss		$(100,000)

  * Allocated costs that would be redistributed to other product
    lines if digital watches were dropped.
  ** No resale value.

Should the company retain or drop the digital watch line? The solution can be obtained by two different approaches.

DROP OR RETAIN A SEGMENT (cont'd)

Approach #1:

If by dropping digital watches the company is able to avoid more in fixed costs than it loses in contribution margin, then it will be better off if the line is eliminated.

The solution would be:

Contribution margin lost if digital watches are dropped		$(300,000)
Less fixed costs that can be avoided:		
Salary of the line manager	$ 90,000	
Advertising—direct	100,000	
Rent—factory space	70,000	260,000
Net disadvantage of dropping the line .		$(40,000)

The digital watch line should not be dropped. If it is dropped, the company will be $40,000 worse off each year. Note the following points:

- Depreciation on equipment with no resale value is not relevant to the decision since it is a sunk cost and therefore is not avoidable.

- General factory overhead and general administrative expense are both allocated costs that would not be avoided if the digital watch line were dropped. These costs would be reallocated to other product lines.

DROP OR RETAIN A SEGMENT (cont'd)

Approach #2:

The solution can also be obtained by preparing comparative income statements showing results with and without the digital watch line.

	Keep Digital Watches	Drop Digital Watches	Difference: Net Income Increase or (Decrease)
Sales	$ 500,000	$ -0-	$(500,000)
Less variable expenses:			
Variable manuf. expense .	120,000	-0-	120,000
Freight out	5,000	-0-	5,000
Commissions	75,000	-0-	75,000
Total variable expenses . . .	200,000	-0-	200,000
Contribution margin	300,000	-0-	(300,000)
Less fixed expenses:			
General factory overhead .	60,000	60,000	-0-
Salary of line manager . . .	90,000	-0-	90,000
Depreciation	50,000	50,000	-0-
Advertising—direct	100,000	-0-	100,000
Rent—factory space . . .	70,000	-0-	70,000
General admin. expense . .	30,000	30,000	-0-
Total fixed expenses	400,000	140,000	260,000
Net loss	$(100,000)	$(140,000)	$ (40,000)

MAKE OR BUY DECISION

A decision concerning whether an item should be produced internally or purchased from an outside supplier is called a "make or buy" decision.

EXAMPLE: Essex Company is presently making a part that is used in one of its products. The unit cost to make the part is:

Direct materials	$ 9
Direct labor	5
Variable overhead	1
Depreciation of special equipment*	3
Supervisor's salary	2
General factory overhead**	10
Total cost per unit	$30

    * No resale value
    ** Allocated on the basis of direct labor hours.

The costs above are based on 20,000 parts produced each year. An outside supplier has offered to provide the 20,000 parts at a cost of only $25 per part. Should this offer be accepted?

In deciding whether to accept the outside supplier's offer, the company should isolate the relevant costs of making the part. To do this, the company will need to eliminate:
- the sunk costs.
- the future costs that will not differ between making or buying the parts.

MAKE OR BUY DECISION (cont'd)

The solution to Essex Company's make or buy decision follows:

	Production Cost Per Unit	Total Differential Costs of 20,000 units Make	Buy
Outside purchase price . . .			$500,000
Direct materials	$ 9	$180,000	
Direct labor	5	100,000	
Variable overhead	1	20,000	
Depreciation of equipment . .	3	—	
Supervisor's Salary	2	40,000	
General factory overhead . .	10	—	
Total costs	$30	$340,000	$500,000

This solution assumes that none of the general factory overhead costs will be saved if the parts are purchased from the outside; these costs would be reallocated to other items made by the company.

UTILIZATION OF SCARCE RESOURCES

Firms often face the problem of deciding how scarce resources are going to be utilized. For example, a particular machine may not have enough capacity to satisfy the current demand for all of the company's products. How should the company decide which products to make?

Usually, fixed costs are not affected by the decision of which products should be emphasized in the short run. All of the machines are in place— it is just a question of how they should be used.

When fixed costs are unaffected by the choice of which product to emphasize, we can focus on the total contribution margin. In this situation, maximizing the total contribution margin will also maximize total profits.

In decisions involving the use of a scarce resource, we would like to know how much contribution margin is generated by using the resource to make each product. The contribution margin per unit of the scarce resource provides this key piece of information.

When the scarce resource is a machine or a particular work center, it is called a <u>bottleneck</u>.

UTILIZATION OF SCARCE RESOURCES (cont'd)

EXAMPLE: Ensign Company manufactures two products, X and Y. Selected data on the products follow:

	X	Y
Selling price per unit	$60	$50
Less variable expenses per unit	36	35
Contribution margin	$24	$15
Contribution margin ratio	40%	30%
Current demand per week (units)	2,000	2,200
Processing time required on Machine N34 per unit	1 min.	.5 min.

Machine N34 is the bottleneck in the plant. There is excess capacity on all of the other machines—Machine N34 is the only machine that is being used to 100% of its capacity. Machine N34 is available for 2,400 minutes per week, which is not enough capacity to satisfy demand for both product X and product Y. Should the company focus its efforts on product X or product Y?

The contribution margin per unit of the scarce resource

	X	Y
Contribution margin per unit (a)	$24	$15
Time required to produce one unit (b)	1 min.	.5 min.
Contribution margin per minute (a)÷(b)	$24/min.	$30/min.

UTILIZATION OF SCARCE RESOURCES (cont'd)

Product Y should be emphasized. A minute of processing time on Machine N34 can be used to make 1 unit of Product X, with a contribution margin of $24, or 2 units of Product Y, with a combined contribution margin of $30.

If there are no other considerations (such as pleasing an important customer), the best plan would be to produce to meet current demand for Product Y and then use any capacity that remains to make Product X.

Allotting the scarce resource

Total time available on Machine N34	2,400 min.
Planned production and sales of Product Y .	2,200 units
Time required to process one unit	X .5 min.
Total time required to make Product Y . . .	1,100 min.
Time available to process Product X	1,300 min.
Time required to process one unit	÷ 1 min.
Planned production and sales of Product X .	1,300 units

Total contribution margin

	X	Y	Total
Planned production and sales (units)	1,300	2,200	
Contribution margin per unit	X $24	X $15	
Total contribution margin	$31,200	33,000	$64,200

UTILIZATION OF SCARCE RESOURCES (cont'd)

MANAGING CONSTRAINTS

A key to increased profits is to figure out ways to process more sellable units through the bottleneck. There are many ways to do this including:
- Produce only what can be sold.
- Pay workers overtime to keep the bottleneck running after normal working hours.
- Shift workers from nonbottleneck areas to the bottleneck.
- Hire more workers or acquire more machines.
- Subcontract some of the production that would use the bottleneck.
- Streamline the production process at the bottleneck to eliminate wasted time.
- Reduce defects.

The potential payoff to effectively managing the constraint can be enormous.

EXAMPLE: Suppose the amount of time Machine N34 is available can be increased by paying the machine's operator to work overtime. Is it likely that running the machine in overtime would be worth the additional cost?

Answer: Since the additional time would be used to make more of Product X, each minute of overtime is worth $24 to the company and hence each hour is worth $1,440 (60 hrs X $24/hr). Since overtime pay is likely to be almost inconsequential relative to this potential payoff, the machine should be run overtime.

JOINT PRODUCT COSTS

Some companies manufacture several end products from a single raw material input. Such products are known as <u>joint products</u>.

- The <u>split-off point</u> is the point in the manufacturing process at which the joint products can be recognized as separate products.

- The term <u>joint product costs</u> is used to describe those costs that are incurred up to the split-off point.

It will always be profitable to continue processing a joint product after the split-off point so long as the incremental revenue from such processing exceeds the incremental processing costs.

In practice, the joint costs incurred up to the split-off point are almost always allocated to the joint products. Extreme caution must be exercised in interpreting these allocated joint costs. They are <u>not</u> relevant in decisions concerning whether joint products should be processed further since they are incurred whether or not there is further processing.

JOINT PRODUCT COSTS (cont'd)

EXAMPLE: NW Sawmill cuts logs from which unfinished lumber and scrap (i.e., sawdust, chips, and bark) are the immediate joint products. The unfinished lumber can be sold "as is" or processed further into finished lumber. The scrap can also be sold "as is" to gardening supply wholesalers or processed further into presto-logs. Data concerning these joint products appear below:

	Per Log	
	Lumber	Scraps
Sales value at the split-off point	$140	$40
Sales value after further processing . . .	270	50
Allocated joint product costs	176	24
Cost of further processing	50	20

Analysis of Sell or Process Further

	Per Log	
	Lumber	Scraps
Sales value after further processing . . .	$270	$50
Sales value at the split-off point	140	40
Incremental revenue	130	10
Cost of further processing	50	20
Profit (loss) from further processing . . .	$80	$(10)

Question: If the sales value of the scraps at the split-off point drops to $20, should they be thrown away?

Answer: No. The allocated joint product cost of $24 will be incurred whether the scraps are thrown away, sold "as is", or processed further and then sold. As long as the scraps can be sold for some price, they should not be thrown away.

PRESENT VALUE CONCEPTS

A dollar today is worth more than a year from now. There are two reasons why this is true.
- Money has a time value.
- The future involves uncertainty.

THEORY OF INTEREST

The time value of money can be shown by the theory of interest formulas. If P dollars are invested today at the interest rate r, then in n years you would have F_n dollars computed as follows:

$$F_n = P(1 + r)^n$$

EXAMPLE: If $100 is invested today at 8% interest, how much will the investment be worth in two years?

$$F_2 = \$100(1 + 0.08)^2$$
$$F_2 = \$116.64$$

The $100 investment earns $16.64 in interest over the two years as follows:

Original deposit	$100.00
Interest—first year ($100 x 0.08)	8.00
Total amount	108.00
Interest—second year ($108 x 0.08)	8.64
Total amount	$116.64

PRESENT AND FUTURE VALUES

The value of an investment can be viewed in two ways. It can viewed either in terms of its value in the future or in terms of its value in the present, as shown below.

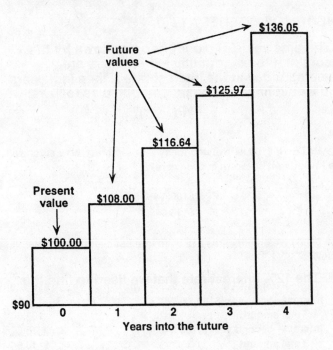

PRESENT VALUE

The <u>present value</u> of any sum to be received in the future can be computed by turning the interest formula around and solving for P:

$$P = \frac{F_n}{(1 + r)^n} \text{ or, } P = F_n\left[\frac{1}{(1 + r)^n}\right]$$

EXAMPLE: A bond will pay off $100 in two years. What is the present value of the $100 if an investor can earn a return of 12% on investments?

$$P = \$100\left[\frac{1}{(1 + 0.12)^2}\right]$$
$$P = \$100 \,(0.797)$$
$$P = \$79.70$$

The following points should be noted:

- The process of finding the present value of a future cash flow is called <u>discounting</u>. We have <u>discounted</u> the $100 to its present value of $79.70.

- The 12% interest rate that we used to find this present value is called the <u>discount rate</u>.

- There are several ways to find the <u>present value factor</u> 0.797:
  - Using the formula (perhaps with the help of a calculator).
  - Using a Present Value Table.

PRESENT VALUE TABLES

Excerpt from Table J-3

Present Value of $1; $P = \dfrac{F_n}{(1 + r)^n}$

Periods ...	10%	12%	14%	...
1	0.909	0.893	0.877	
2	0.826	0.797	0.769	
3	0.751	0.712	0.675	
4	0.683	0.636	0.592	
5	0.621	0.567	0.519	

Note:

- The numbers in the table represent the present value, at the specified discount rate, of $1 received at the end of the specified period.

- The present value can be interpreted as the amount that would have to be put into the bank today at the specified interest rate in order to have accumulate $1 at the end of the specified period.

- The present value factors decrease as one moves down a column. Why?

- The present value factors also decrease as one moves across a row to the right. Why?

PRESENT VALUE TABLES (cont'd)

Some investments involve a series of identical cash flows at the end of each year. Such a stream of equal cash flows is called an <u>annuity</u>.

EXAMPLE: Lacey Company has purchased a tract of land on which a $60,000 payment will be due each year for the next five years. What is the present value of this stream of cash payments when the discount rate is 12%?

Year	Cash Payment	12% Factor (Table J-3)	Present Value
1	$60,000	0.893	$ 53,580
2	60,000	0.797	47,820
3	60,000	0.712	42,720
4	60,000	0.636	38,160
5	60,000	0.567	34,020
		3.605	$216,300

We could have saved ourselves a little work if we had just multiplied the sum of the present value factors by the annual cash payment:

$$3.605 \times \$60,000 = \$216,300$$

We can even avoid having to add together the present value factors by using a Present Value Table for an Annuity. The $60,000 equal cash payments constitute an annuity. The annuity table assumes that the first payment occurs at the end of the first period and then continues for n periods.

PRESENT VALUE TABLES (cont'd)

Excerpt from Table J-4
Present Value of an Annuity of $1 in Arrears

Periods ...	10%	12%	14% ...
1	0.909	0.893	0.877
2	1.736	1.690	1.647
3	2.487	2.402	2.322
4	3.170	3.037	2.914
5	3.791	3.605	3.433

Table J-4 is constructed by adding down the column in Table J-3:

	12%	
Periods	Table J-3	Table J-4
1	0.893	0.893
2	+ 0.797 →	1.690
3	+ 0.712 →	2.402
4	+ 0.636 →	3.037
5	+ 0.567 →	3.605

CAPITAL BUDGETING

 Capital budgeting is concerned with planning
and financing capital outlays for purposes such as
acquiring new equipment.

CAPITAL BUDGETING METHODS

 Capital budgeting methods can be divided into
two groups:
1. Discounted cash flow:
   a. Net present value method.
   b. Time-adjusted rate of return method.
2. Other methods:
   a. Payback method.
   b. Simple rate of return method.

 As the name implies, the discounted cash flow
methods involve discounting cash flows, *not*
accounting net income.

 Typical cash flows:
- Cash outflows:
  - Initial investment.
  - Increased working capital.
  - Repairs and maintenance.
  - Incremental operating costs.
- Cash inflows:
  - Incremental revenues.
  - Reduction in costs.
  - Salvage value.
  - Release of working capital.

NET PRESENT VALUE METHOD

Under the net present value method, the present value of all cash inflows is compared to the present value of all cash outflows caused by an investment project.

EXAMPLE: Harper Company has been offered a five year contract to provide component parts for a large manufacturer. The following information relates to the contract:

1. Costs and revenues due to the contract would be:

Cost of special equipment	$160,000
Working capital required	100,000
Relining of the equipment in three years	30,000
Salvage value of the equipment in five years . .	5,000
Annual revenues and costs:	
Sales revenue from parts	750,000
Cost of parts sold	400,000
Out-of-pocket costs (for salaries,	
shipping, and so forth)	270,000

2. At the end of five years the working capital would be released for use elsewhere.

3. Harper Company uses a discount rate of 10 percent.

Given the above data, should the contract be accepted?

NET PRESENT VALUE METHOD (cont'd)

Sales revenue	$750,000
Cost of parts sold	400,000
Gross margin	350,000
Less out-of-pocket costs . . .	270,000
Annual net cash inflows	$ 80,000

	Year(s)	Cash Flow	10% Factor	Present Value
Investment in equipment	Now	$(160,000)	1.000	$(160,000)
Working capital needed	Now	(100,000)	1.000	(100,000)
Annual net cash inflows	1-5	80,000	3.791	303,280
Relining of equipment	3	(30,000)	0.751	(22,530)
Working capital released	5	100,000	0.621	62,100
Salvage value of equipment	5	5,000	0.621	3,150
Net present value				$ 86,000

TIME ADJUSTED RATE OF RETURN

The <u>time-adjusted rate of return</u>, or <u>internal rate of return</u>, is the interest yield promised by an investment project over its useful life.

The time-adjusted rate of return is computed by finding the discount rate that will cause the net present value of a project to be zero.

EXAMPLE: Decker Company can purchase a new machine at a cost of $104,320 that will save $20,000 per year in cash operating costs. The machine will have a 10-year life. What is the machine's time-adjusted rate of return?

When the future cash flows are the same every year, as in this example, the time-adjusted rate of return can be found by computing the "Factor of the time-adjusted rate of return" as follows:

$$\frac{\text{Investment required}}{\text{Net annual cash flow}} = \frac{\text{Factor of the}}{\text{time-adjusted rate of return}}$$

$$\frac{\$104,320}{\$20,000} = 5.216$$

Looking in Table J-4 for the Present Value of an Annuity and scanning along the 10-period line, we find that the factor of 5.216 corresponds to a rate of return of 14%. We can verify that the time-adjusted rate of return is 14% as follows:

	Year(s)	Amount	14 % Factor	Present Value
Investment required	Now	$(104,320)	1.000	$(104,320)
Annual cost savings	1-10	20,000	5.216	104,320
Net present value				$ -0-

INTERPOLATION

Interpolation is the process of finding odd rates of return that do not appear in published interest tables.

EXAMPLE: Assume that the machine desired by Decker Company costs only $100,000 rather than $104,320. The data are:

Investment required	$100,000
Annual cost savings	$20,000
Life of the machine	10 years

What is the machine's time-adjusted rate of return?

$$\frac{\text{Investment required}}{\text{Net annual cash flow}} = \frac{\text{Factor of the}}{\text{time-adjusted rate of return}}$$

$$\frac{\$100,000}{\$20,000} = 5.000$$

Looking in Table J-4 and scanning along the 10-period line, we find that a factor of 5.000 corresponds to a return of between 14 and 16 percent. To find the return we are after, we will need to interpolate:

	Present Value Factors	
14% factor	5.216	5.216
True factor	5.000	
16% factor	_____	4.833
Difference	0.216	0.383

$$\text{Time-adjusted rate of return} = 14\% + \left(\frac{0.216}{0.383} \times 2\%\right) = 15.1\%$$

COST OF CAPITAL AS A SCREENING TOOL

- Businesses typically use their <u>cost of capital</u> as the discount rate in capital budgeting decisions. The cost of capital is the overall cost to the organization of obtaining investment funds, including the cost of both debt and equity sources.

- The cost of capital can be used to screen out undesirable investment projects:

    Net present value screening method. The cost of capital is used as the discount rate when computing the net present value of a project. Any project with a negative net present value is rejected unless there is some other overriding factor.

    Time-adjusted rate of return screening method. The cost of capital is compared to the time-adjusted rate of return of the project. Any project with a time-adjusted rate of return less than the cost of capital is rejected unless there is some other overriding factor.

NET PRESENT VALUE:
TOTAL-COST APPROACH

White Company is trying to decide whether to remodel an old car wash or remove it entirely and install a new one in its place. The company uses a discount rate of 10%. Relevant data follow:

	New Car Wash	Old Car Wash
Annual revenues	$90,000	$70,000
Annual cash operating costs	30,000	25,000
Net annual cash inflows	$60,000	$45,000

	Year(s)	Cash Flows	10% Factor	Present Value
Install new car wash:				
Initial investment	Now	$(300,000)	1.000	$(300,000)
Replacement of brushes	6	(50,000)	0.564	(28,200)
Net annual cash inflows	1-10	60,000	6.145	368,700
Salvage of old equipment	Now	40,000	1.000	40,000
Salvage of new equipment	10	7,000	0.386	2,702
Net present value				$ 83,202
Remodel old car wash:				
Initial investment	Now	$(175,000)	1.000	$(175,000)
Replacement of brushes	6	(80,000)	0.564	(45,120)
Net annual cash inflows	1-10	45,000	6.145	276,525
Salvage of old equipment	10	-0-	0.386	-0-
Net present value				$ 56,405
Net present value in favor of the new car wash				$ 26,797

NET PRESENT VALUE:
INCREMENTAL-COST APPROACH

When only two alternatives are being considered, the incremental-cost approach offers a simpler and more direct route to a decision than the total-cost approach.

The data on White Company's car washes are shown below in incremental format. The table considers only those cash flows that would change if the new car wash were installed (i.e., only the relevant cash flows).

	Year(s)	Cash Flows	10% Factor	Present Value
Incremental investment required for the new car wash	Now	$(125,000)	1.000	$(125,000)
Cost avoided on brush replacements	6	30,000	0.564	16,920
Increased net annual cash inflows	1-10	15,000	6.145	92,175
Salvage of old equipment	Now	40,000	1.000	40,000
Salvage of new equipment	10	7,000	0.386	2,702
Net present value in favor of the new car wash				$ 26,797

LEAST COST DECISIONS:
TOTAL-COST APPROACH

In decisions where revenues are not directly involved, the manager should choose the alternative that has the least total cost from a present value perspective.

EXAMPLE: Home Furniture Company is trying to decide whether to overhaul an old delivery truck or purchase a new one. The company uses a discount rate of 10%. Using a total cost approach, the analysis would be conducted as follows:

	Year(s)	Cash Flows	10% Factor	Present Value
Buy the new truck:				
Purchase cost	Now	$(21,000)	1.000	$(21,000)
Annual cash operating costs	1-5	(6,000)	3.791	(22,746)
Salvage value of old truck	Now	9,000	1.000	9,000
Salvage value of new truck	5	3,000	0.621	1,863
Present value				$(32,883)
Keep the old truck:				
Overhaul cost	Now	$(4,500)	1.000	$(4,500)
Annual cash operating costs	1-5	(10,000)	3.791	(37,910)
Salvage value of old truck	5	250	0.621	155
Present value				$(42,255)
Net present value in favor of purchasing the new truck				$ 9,372

LEAST COST DECISIONS:
INCREMENTAL-COST APPROACH

Least cost decisions can also be made using the incremental-cost approach.

Data relating to Home Furniture Company's delivery truck decision are presented below focusing only on incremental costs. Only those cash flows that would change if the new truck were purchased are included in the analysis.

	Year(s)	Cash Flows	10% Factor	Present Value
Incremental cost to purchase the new truck	Now	$(16,500)	1.000	$(16,500)
Savings in annual cash operating costs	1-5	4,000	3.791	15,164
Salvage value of old truck	Now	9,000	1.000	9,000
Difference in salvage value in 5 years	5	2,750	0.621	1,708
Net present value in favor of purchasing the new truck				$ 9,372

INVESTMENTS IN AUTOMATED EQUIPMENT

Investments in automated equipment differ in several ways from investments in other types of equipment.

COST OF AUTOMATION

The cost of automating a process is usually much greater than the cost of purchasing conventional equipment. The front-end investment in robots and other hardware often constitutes less than half of the total cost to automate. The costs of engineering, software development, and implementation of the system can equal or exceed the cost of the equipment itself.

BENEFITS OF AUTOMATION

Identifying and measuring the benefits that automated equipment will provide is a difficult task — particularly since many of those benefits are intangible.

BENEFITS FROM AUTOMATION (cont'd)

TANGIBLE BENEFITS:

1. *Reduced direct labor cost.*

2. *Reduced inventory cost.*

3. *Reduced costs of dealing with defective units.*

Note that these tangible benefits represent potential cost savings.

INTANGIBLE BENEFITS:

1. *Faster throughput time.*

2. *Increased manufacturing flexibility.*

3. *Faster response to market shifts.*

4. *Increased learning effects.*

5. *Avoiding capital decay (i.e., loss of market share).*

6. *Higher quality of output.*

Note that most of the intangible benefits are potential revenue enhancements and are particularly difficult to estimate.

DECISION FRAMEWORK FOR AUTOMATED EQUIPMENT

The following steps provide a decision framework for purchases of automated equipment:

1. Determine the long-term strategic goals and objectives of the company and a manufacturing strategy that will allow these goals and objectives to be achieved.

2. List all the expected benefits and costs associated with the automated equipment under consideration.

3. Quantify those items from step 2 that can be readily estimated.

4. Determine the net present value or time-adjusted rate of return for those items quantified in step 3. These computations may justify acquisition of the equipment. If not, then proceed to step 5.

5. Try to quantify the intangible benefits from step 2, and recompute the net present value or time-adjusted rate of return. As an alternate step, determine the amount of additional cash flow per year that would be needed to make the project acceptable, and then ask the question, "Are the intangible benefits worth at least this much to the company?" If so, the project should be accepted; if not, it should be rejected.

DECISION FRAMEWORK FOR AUTOMATED EQUIPMENT (cont'd)

Example: Assume that a company is considering buying automated equipment that would have a 10 year useful life. By applying steps 3-4 and a 10% discount rate, the equipment shows a negative net present value of $491,600. The amount of additional cash flow per year that would be needed to make the project acceptable could be calculated as follows:

Net present value (negative) . . . . $(491,600)
Present value factor for a 10% annuity
    over 10 periods 6.145

$$\frac{\text{-Net present value of project}}{\text{Present value of an annuity}} = \frac{\text{Required annual value}}{\text{of intangible benefits}}$$

$$\frac{-(-491,600)}{6.145} = \$80,000$$

If the intangible benefits from the new equipment are worth at least $80,000 per year, the machine should be purchased.

To verify this, suppose the intangible benefits are worth exactly $80,000 per year. The present value of these benefits would be $491,600 = 6.145 X $80,000. This would be precisely enough to offset the negative net present value of $491,600 when the intangible benefits are not included. Therefore, if the intangible benefits are worth more than $80,000 per year, the net present value of the project, *including the intangible benefits*, would be positive.

OTHER CAPITAL BUDGETING METHODS

Two other popular methods of making capital budgeting decisions do not involve discounting cash flows. They are the <u>payback method</u> and the <u>simple rate of return method</u>.

THE PAYBACK METHOD

- The <u>payback period</u> is the length of time that it takes for an investment to recoup its initial cost out of the cash receipts that it generates.

- The basic premise of the payback method is that the quicker the cost of an investment can be recovered, the better the investment is.

- The payback method is most appropriate when considering projects whose useful lives are short and unpredictable.

- The payback period is expressed in years. When the same cash flow occurs every year, the following formula can be used:

$$\frac{\text{Investment Required}}{\text{Net Annual Cash Inflow}} = \text{Payback Period}$$

THE PAYBACK METHOD (cont'd)

EXAMPLE: Myers Company wants to install an espresso bar in place of several coffee vending machines in one of its stores. The company estimates that incremental annual revenues and expenses associated with the espresso bar would be:

Sales		$100,000
Less variable expenses		30,000
Contribution margin		70,000
Less fixed expenses:		
Insurance	$ 9,000	
Salaries	26,000	
Depreciation	15,000	50,000
Net income		$ 20,000

Equipment for the espresso bar would cost $150,000 and have a 10-year life. The old vending machines could be sold now for a $10,000 salvage value. The company requires a payback of 5 years or less on all investments.

Net income (above)	$20,000
Add: Noncash deduction for depreciation . .	15,000
Net annual cash inflow	$35,000
Investment in the espresso bar	$150,000
Deduct: Salvage value of old machines . . .	10,000
Investment required	$140,000

$$\frac{\text{Investment Required}}{\text{Net Annual Cash Inflow}} = \text{Payback Period}$$

$$\frac{\$140,000}{\$35,000} = 4.0 \text{ years}$$

SIMPLE RATE OF RETURN METHOD

Unlike other capital budgeting methods, the simple rate of return method does not focus on cash flows. Rather, it focuses on accounting net income. The formula is:

$$\text{Simple Rate of Return} = \frac{\text{Incremental Revenue} - \text{Incremental Expenses}}{\text{Initial Investment}}$$

Note that incremental revenue and incremental expenses are not necessarily the same as incremental cash inflows and outflows. For example, depreciation should be included as part of incremental expenses but not as part of incremental cash outflows.

EXAMPLE: Refer to the data for Myers Company on the preceding page. What is the simple rate of return on the espresso bar?

Incremental revenue $100,000
Incremental expenses 80,000
Initial investment 140,000

$$\text{Simple Rate of Return} = \frac{\$100,000 - \$80,000}{\$140,000} = 14.3\%$$

The simple rate of return method is not recommended for a variety of reasons, the most important of which is that it ignores the time value of money.

CAPITAL BUDGETING AND TAXES

The effects of income taxes on cash flows must be considered in capital budgeting decisions when an organization is subject to income taxes.

AFTER TAX COST

A cash expense net of its tax effect is known as an <u>after-tax cost</u>.

EXAMPLE: Companies X and Y are identical except that X has a $40,000 annual cash expense for a training program.

	Company X	*Company Y*
Sales	<u>$250,000</u>	<u>$250,000</u>
Less expenses:		
Salaries, insurance, other	150,000	150,000
Training program	<u>40,000</u>	<u>—</u>
Total expenses	<u>190,000</u>	<u>150,000</u>
Income before taxes	60,000	100,000
Less income taxes (30%)	<u>18,000</u>	<u>30,000</u>
Net income	<u>$ 42,000</u>	<u>$ 70,000</u>

After-tax cost of the training program $28,000

The following formula shows the after-tax cost of any tax-deductible cash expense:

(1 — Tax rate) X Cash expense = After-tax cost
(1 — 0.30) X $40,000   = $28,000

AFTER-TAX BENEFIT

A cash receipt net of its tax effects is known as an <u>after-tax benefit</u>. The formula to compute the after-tax benefit from any taxable cash receipt is:

(1 —Tax rate) X Cash receipt = After-tax benefit

EXAMPLE: Company A receives $80,000 per year from subleasing part of its office space. If the tax rate is 30%, what is the after-tax benefit from subleasing the space?

(1 - 0.30) X $80,000 = $56,000

If the same cash receipts and cash expenses recur each year, the expenses can be deducted from the receipts and the difference multiplied by (1 —Tax rate).

EXAMPLE: Company B can invest in a project that would provide cash receipts of $400,000 per year. Cash operating expenses would be $280,000 per year. If the tax rate is 30%, what is the after-tax benefit (cash inflow) each year from the project?

Annual cash receipts	$400,000
Annual cash operating expenses .	280,000
Annual net cash inflow	120,000
Multiply by (1 —0.30)	X 0.70
Annual after-tax net cash inflow . .	$ 84,000

DEPRECIATION TAX SHIELD

Although depreciation is not a cash flow, it does have an impact on the amount of income taxes that a firm will pay. Depreciation deductions shield revenues from taxation (called a <u>depreciation tax shield</u>) and thereby reduce tax payments.

EXAMPLE: Companies A and B are identical except that A has a $60,000 annual depreciation expense:

	Company A	*Company B*
Sales	$500,000	$500,000
Less expenses:		
Cash operating expenses	340,000	340,000
Depreciation expense	60,000	—
Total expenses	400,000	340,000
Income before taxes	100,000	160,000
Less income taxes(30%)	30,000	48,000
Net income	$ 70,000	$112,000

As a result of the depreciation deduction, although A has less net income it has a greater cash inflow:

Cash inflow from operations:		
Net income, as above	$ 70,000	$112,000
Add: Depreciation	60,000	—
Net cash inflow	$130,000	$112,000

The tax savings provided by the depreciation tax shield can be computed by the following formula:

Tax rate X Depreciation deduction = Tax savings
0.30 X $60,000 = $18,000

MODIFIED ACCELERATED COST RECOVERY SYSTEM (MACRS)
(Exhibit 15-4)

MACRS Property Class and Depreciation Method	Useful Life of Assets Included in This Class	Examples of Assets Included in This Class
3-year property 200% declining balance	4 years or less	Most small tools are included; the law specifically *excludes* autos and light trucks from this property class.
5-year property 200% declining balance	More than 4 years to less than 10 years	Autos and light trucks, computers, typewriters, copiers, duplicating equipment, heavy general-purpose trucks, and research and experimentation equipment are included.
7-year property 200% declining balance	10 years or more to less than 16 years	Office furniture and fixtures, and most items of machinery and equipment used in production are included.
10-year property 200% declining balance	16 years or more to less than 20 years	Various machinery and equipment, such as that used in petroleum distilling and refining and in the milling of grain, are included.
15-year property 150% declining balance	20 years or more to less than 25 years	Sewage treatment plants, telephone and electrical distribution facilities, and land improvements are included.
20-year property 150% declining balance	25 years or more	Service stations and other real property with a useful life of less than 27.5 years are included.
27.5-year property Straight line	Not applicable	All residential rental property is included.
31.5-year property Straight line	Not applicable	All nonresidential real property is included.

MACRS (cont'd)
(Exhibit 15-5)

Year	Property Class					
	3-Year	5-Year	7-Year	10-Year	15-Year	20-Year
1.	33.3%	20.0%	14.3%	10.0%	5.0%	3.8%
2.	44.5	32.0	24.5	18.0	9.5	7.2
3.	14.8*	19.2	17.5	14.4	8.6	6.7
4.	7.4	11.5*	12.5	11.5	7.7	6.2
5.		11.5	8.9*	9.2	6.9	5.7
6.		5.8	8.9	7.4	6.2	5.3
7.			8.9	6.6*	5.9*	4.9
8.			4.5	6.6	5.9	4.5*
9.				6.5	5.9	4.5
10.				6.5	5.9	4.5
11.				3.3	5.9	4.5
12.					5.9	4.5
13.					5.9	4.5
14.					5.9	4.5
15.					5.9	4.5
16.					3.0	4.4
17.						4.4
18.						4.4
19.						4.4
20.						4.4
21.						2.2
Total	100.0%	100.0%	100.0%	100.0%	100.0%	100.0%

* Denotes the year of changeover to straight-line depreciation.

MACRS TABLES

The MACRS tables are constructed using two conventions:

- It is assumed that all assets enter service halfway through the first year and leave service halfway through the last year. This is called the <u>half-year convention</u>.

- The depreciation method changes from an accelerated method to the straight line method in the year that the straight line depreciation begins to exceed the accelerated depreciation.

Salvage value is not deducted from the cost of an asset when computing depreciation under the MACRS system.

EXAMPLE: Mason Company purchased a light truck at a cost of $30,000 in March. The truck's useful life is 7 years and it has an estimated salvage value of $2,000.

Year	Cost	MACRS %	Depreciation
1	$30,000	20.0%	$ 6,000
2	30,000	32.0	9,600
3	30,000	19.2	5,760
4	30,000	11.5	3,450
5	30,000	11.5	3,450
6	30,000	5.8	1,740
Total		100.0%	$30,000

MACRS STRAIGHT LINE

A company can elect to compute depreciation deductions using the optional straight-line method. If this method is elected, depreciation is spread over the asset's property class life.

As with the MACRS tables, when the optional straight-line method is used the half-year convention must be observed and salvage value is not considered.

Example: Assume the same data as before for the Mason Company, but the company elects to use the optional straight-line method to depreciate the truck. Since the truck's useful life is seven years, it is in the 5-year property class and will be depreciated as follows:

$30,000 ÷ 5 years = $6,000 per year.

Year	Straight-line Depreciation
1988 (half year's depreciation)	$ 3,000
1989	6,000
1990	6,000
1991	6,000
1992	6,000
1993 (half year's depreciation)	3,000
Total	$30,000

CAPITAL BUDGETING AND TAXES — EXAMPLE

The concepts of after-tax cost, after-tax benefit and depreciation tax shield are integrated in the following example:

EXAMPLE: Martin Company has an investment opportunity that would involve the following cash flows:

Cost of new equipment	$400,000
Working capital required	80,000
Net annual cash receipts for 8 years	100,000
Equipment repairs in 4 years	40,000
Salvage value of equipment	50,000

The following additional information is available:

- Equipment's useful life: 8 years
- MACRS property class: _?_ year
- After-tax cost of capital: 10%
- Income tax rate: 30%

ANALYSIS OF THE PROJECT

	Year(s)	(1) Amount	(2) Tax effect	After-tax cash flows (1) x (2)	10% Factor	Present value
Cost of new equipment	Now	$(400,000)	—	$(400,000)	1.000	$(400,000)
Working capital needed	Now	(80,000)	—	(80,000)	1.000	(80,000)
Net annual cash receipts	1-8	100,000	1-0.30	70,000	5.335	373,450
Equipment repairs	4	(40,000)	1-0.30	(28,000)	0.683	(19,124)

Depreciation deductions: MACRS (5-year property class)

	Cost	%	Dep'n						
1	$400,000	20.0	$ 80,000	1	80,000	0.30	24,000	0.909	21,816
2	400,000	32.0	128,000	2	128,000	0.30	38,400	0.826	31,718
3	400,000	19.2	76,800	3	76,800	0.30	23,040	0.751	17,303
4	400,000	11.5	46,000	4	46,000	0.30	13,800	0.683	9,425
5	400,000	11.5	46,000	5	46,000	0.30	13,800	0.621	8,570
6	400,000	5.8	23,200	6	23,200	0.30	6,960	0.564	3,925

	Year(s)	(1) Amount	(2) Tax effect	After-tax cash flows (1) x (2)	10% Factor	Present value
Salvage value of equipment	8	50,000	1-0.30	35,000	0.467	16,345
Release of working capital	8	80,000	—	80,000	0.467	37,360
Net present value						$ 20,788

RANKING INVESTMENT PROJECTS

Ranking investment projects involves <u>preference decisions</u>. Preference decisions come after screening decisions and are concerned with deciding which of the acceptable projects is best.

TIME ADJUSTED RATE OF RETURN

When using the time-adjusted rate of return method to rank competing investment projects, the preference rule is: The higher the time-adjusted rate of return, the more desirable the project.

NET PRESENT VALUE

The net present value of one investment project cannot be compared directly to the net present value of another investment project unless the projects are of equal size.

EXAMPLE: Dexter Company is considering two investment projects, as shown below:

	Project A	Project B
Investment required	$(600,000)	$(300,000)
Present value of cash inflows	690,000	380,000
Net present value	$ 90,000	$ 80,000

Although A has a higher net present value than B, it is difficult to compare the projects since they are not equal in size.

NET PRESENT VALUE (cont'd)

The <u>profitability index</u> permits comparisons of different sized projects.

$$\frac{\text{Present value of cash inflows}}{\text{Investment required}} = \text{Profitability index}$$

Project A: $\dfrac{\$690,000}{\$600,000} = 1.15$

Project B: $\dfrac{\$380,000}{\$300,000} = 1.27$

The profitability indexes show that B will generate $1.27 of cash inflow for each dollar of investment, whereas A will generate only $1.15 of cash inflow for each dollar of investment. Thus, B is more desirable than A.

When using the net present value method to rank competing investment projects, the preference rule is: The higher the profitability index, the more desirable the project.

SERVICE DEPARTMENT COSTS

Service department costs are allocated to operating departments for three reasons:

1. To help evaluate performance in operating departments.

2. To help measure profitability in operating departments.

3. To develop overhead rates in the operating departments. These rates are used for costing products and billing services.

First Stage
Service department costs are allocated to operating departments.

Second Stage
Operating department overhead costs, plus allocated service department costs, are applied to products and services by means of departmental overhead rates.

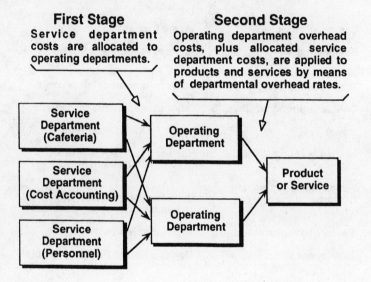

BASES COMMONLY USED IN ALLOCATING SERVICE DEPARTMENT COSTS

Service Department	Allocation bases
Laundry	Pounds of laundry; number of items processed
Airport ground services	Number of flights
Cafeteria	Number of employees
Medical facilities	Cases handled; number of employees; hours worked
Materials handling	Hours of service; volume handled
Data processing	CPU minutes; lines printed; storage used
Custodial services	Square footage occupied
Engineering	Services rendered; labor hours
Production planning and control	Services rendered; labor hours
Cost accounting	Labor hours; clients or patients
Power	Usage (in kwh); machine capacity
Human resources	Number of employees; labor turnover; training hours
Receiving, shipping, and stores	Units handled; number of requisitions; space occupied
Factory administration	Total labor hours
Maintenance	Machine hours; total labor hours

RECIPROCAL SERVICES

Many service departments provide services for each other, as well as for operating departments. Services that service departments provide to each other are known as <u>reciprocal</u> or <u>interdepartmental</u> services.

There are three approaches to allocating the costs of service departments: the <u>direct method</u>, the <u>step method</u>, and the <u>reciprocal method</u>.

- The <u>direct method</u> ignores the reciprocal services that service departments provide to each other and allocates service department costs directly to operating departments.

- The <u>step method</u> provides for the allocation of a service department's costs to some other service departments, as well as to operating departments. This sequential method takes into account many of the reciprocal services, but not all of them.

- Unlike the direct and step methods, the <u>reciprocal</u> method fully accounts for all of the reciprocal services. However, the mathematics of the reciprocal method are relatively complex and so it is seldom used.

GRAPHIC ILLUSTRATION OF THE STEP METHOD
(Exhibit 16-3)

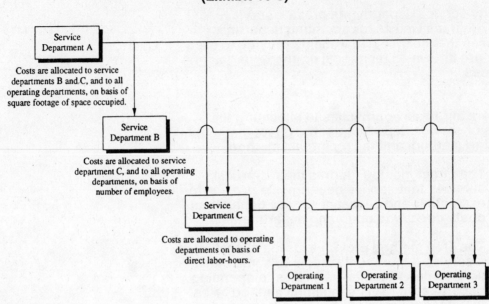

Service
Department A

Costs are allocated to service
departments B and C, and to all
operating departments, on basis of
square footage of space occupied.

Service
Department B

Costs are allocated to service
department C, and to all operating
departments, on basis of
number of employees.

Service
Department C

Costs are allocated to operating
departments on basis of
direct labor-hours.

Operating
Department 1

Operating
Department 2

Operating
Department 3

STEP METHOD

When allocating costs by the step method, the sequence begins with the department that provides the greatest amount of service to other departments. Assume the following data:

	Personnel	Custodial Services	Machining	Assembly	Total
Overhead costs	$720,000	$180,000	$ 970,000	$ 630,000	$2,500,000
Number of employees	20	10	100	50	180
Space occupied-square feet . .	9,000	6,000	30,000	70,000	115,000
Overhead cost before allocations	$720,000	$180,000	$ 970,000	$630,000	$2,500,000
Allocations:					
Personnel costs (1/16; 10/16; 5/16) *	(720,000)	45,000	450,000	225,000	
Custodial services costs (3/10; 7/10)**		(225,000)	67,500	157,500	
Overhead cost after allocations	$ -0-	$ -0-	$1,487,500	$1,012,500	$2,500,000

* Based on: 10 + 100 + 50 = 160. (Alternatively: $720,000 ÷ 160 = $4,500/employee.)

** Based on: 30,000 + 70,000 = 100,000. (Alternatively: $225,000 ÷ 100,000 = $2.25/sq. ft.)

DIRECT METHOD

Although the direct method is simpler than the step method, it is less accurate since it ignores interdepartmental services. Again assume the following data:

	Personnel	Custodial Services	Machining	Assembly	Total
Overhead costs	$720,000	$180,000	$ 970,000	$630,000	$2,500,000
Number of employees	20	10	100	50	180
Space occupied—square feet .	9,000	6,000	30,000	70,000	115,000
Overhead cost before allocations	$720,000	$180,000	$ 970,000	$ 630,000	$2,500,000
Allocations:					
Personnel costs (2/3; 1/3)* . .	(720,000)	—	480,000	240,000	
Custodial services costs (3/10; 7/10)**		(180,000)	54,000	126,000	
Overhead cost after allocations	$ -0-	$ -0-	$1,504,000	$996,000	$2,500,000

* Based on: 100 + 50 = 150. (Alternatively: $720,000 ÷ 150 = $4,800/employee.)

** Based on: 30,000 + 70,000 = 100,000. (Alternatively: $180,000 ÷ 100,000 = $1.80/sq. ft.)

ALLOCATING COSTS BY BEHAVIOR

Whenever possible, service department costs should be separated into fixed and variable classifications and allocated separately using the following guidelines:

- Variable costs should be charged at a budgeted rate based on the activity that causes the cost. (If actual rates are used, the operating departments are implicitly held responsible for how well the service departments control spending.)

  - Allocations at the beginning of the period:

    Budgeted rate X Budgeted activity =
        Cost allocated

  - Allocations at the end of the period:

    Budgeted rate X Actual activity =
        Cost allocated

- Fixed costs should be allocated to consuming departments in predetermined lump-sum amounts, using budgeted cost.

  - Fixed costs are incurred to provide capacity.

  - The lump-sum amount going to each department should be in proportion to its demands for capacity (the department's peak-period or long-run average needs).

ALLOCATION EXAMPLE

Implementation of the allocation guidelines is illustrated below.

EXAMPLE: White Company has a Maintenance Department and two operating departments: Cutting and Assembly. Variable maintenance costs are budgeted at $0.60 per machine hour. Fixed maintenance costs are budgeted at $200,000 per year. Data relating to machine hours for next year follow:

	Peak-Load Hours	Budgeted Hours	Actual Hours
Cutting Department . .	90,000	75,000	80,000
Assembly Department .	60,000	50,000	40,000
Total hours	150,000	125,000	120,000

The amount of Maintenance Department cost that would be allocated to each operating department at the beginning of the year would be:

	Cutting Department	Assembly Department
Variable cost allocation:		
$0.60 x 75,000 hours	$ 45,000	
$0.60 X 50,000 hours		$ 30,000
Fixed cost allocation:*		
$200,000 X 60%	120,000	
$200,000 X 40%		80,000
Total cost allocated	$165,000	$110,000

* Based on peak-period hours.

The above allocations would be included in the flexible budgets of the operating departments.

ALLOCATION EXAMPLE (cont'd)

At the end of the year the management of White Company may wish to make a second allocation, this time based on actual activity. Ordinarily, the amounts charged to the operating departments for services will be based on these end-of-period allocations.

Assume that actual Maintenance Department costs for the year were: variable, $0.65 per machine hour ($78,000); fixed, $210,000.

	Cutting Department	Assembly Department
Variable cost allocation:		
$0.60 X 80,000 hours	$ 48,000	
$0.60 x 40,000 hours		$ 24,000
Fixed cost allocation:		
$200,000 X 60%	120,000	
$200,000 X 40%		80,000
Total cost allocated	$168,000	$104,000

Note that the variable costs are allocated according to the budgeted rate per hour, but using the actual activity, and that the fixed costs are allocated according to the original budgeted amount and peak-period demand. Thus, some of the actual year-end costs will not be allocated (or charged out), as shown below:

	Variable	Fixed
Actual costs incurred	$78,000	$210,000
Costs allocated above	72,000*	200,000
Spending variance—not allocated	$ 6,000	$ 10,000

* $0.60 x 120,000 actual hours = $72,000.

THE STATEMENT OF CASH FLOWS

PURPOSE

The purpose of the statement of cash flows is to show the major activities that have provided and used cash during a period.

DEFINITION OF CASH

For purposes of the cash flow statement, cash is broadly defined to include both cash itself and cash equivalents. <u>Cash equivalents</u> consist of short-term, highly liquid investments such as treasury bills, commercial paper, and money market funds.

ORGANIZATION OF THE STATEMENT

The statement of cash flows is divided into three sections, consisting of:

1. Operating activities.

2. Investing activities.

3. Financing activities.

OPERATING ACTIVITIES

General rule: Any transactions that enter into the determination of net income are classified as operating activities. These transactions include:

Cash receipts from:

- Sale of goods or services.

- Interest (from all sources).

- Dividends (on stock of other companies).

- Miscellaneous income, such as from rentals.

Cash payments to:

- Suppliers for purchases of inventory.

- Employees for services.

- Others for insurance, utilities, rent, etc.

- Creditors for interest on debt.

- Government agencies for taxes.

INVESTING ACTIVITIES

General rule: Any transactions that are involved in acquiring or disposing of non-current assets are classified as investing activities. These transactions include:

Cash provided by:

- Sale of property, plant, and equipment

- Sales of securities that are not cash equivalents.

- Collections on a loan made to others.

Cash used to:

- Purchase property, plant, and equipment.

- Purchase securities that are not cash equivalents.

- Lend money to others.

FINANCING ACTIVITIES

General rule: Any transactions (other than the payment of interest) that involve borrowing from creditors and any transactions (except stock dividends and stock splits) involving the owners of the company are classified as financing activities. These transactions include:

Cash provided by:

- **Borrowing from creditors (other than accounts payable).**

- **Sale of capital stock to owners.**

Cash used to:

- **Retire notes, bonds, mortgages, etc.**

- **Repurchase stock from owners.**

- **Pay cash dividends to owners.**

CASH PROVIDED BY OPERATIONS

The net cash flow arising from operations is referred to as the <u>net cash provided by operating activities</u>. This figure can be computed by either the <u>direct method</u> or the <u>indirect method</u>.

DIRECT METHOD

Under the direct method, the income statement is reconstructed on a cash basis from top to bottom. Operating cash outflows are subtracted from operating cash inflows to arrive at net cash flow from operating activities.

INDIRECT METHOD

Under the indirect method, the cash provided by operations is computed by starting with net income and adjusting the net income figure to a cash basis. This needs to be done because of differences between operating cash inflows and revenues and between operating cash outflows and expenses.

GENERAL MODEL—INDIRECT METHOD

Add (+) or
Deduct (−)
to Adjust
Net Income

Net income . . . .   **$XXX**

Adjustments needed to convert net income to a cash basis:

   Depreciation, depletion, and amortization expense   .   **+**

   Add (deduct) changes in current asset accounts
      affecting revenue or expense:
   Increase in the account   . . . .   **−**
   Decrease in the account   . . . .   **+**

   Add (deduct) changes in current liability accounts
      affecting revenue or expense:
   Increase in the account   . . . .   **+**
   Decrease in the account   . . . .   **−**

   Add (deduct) gains or losses on sales of assets:
   Gain on sales of assets   . . . .   **−**
   Losses on sales of assets   . . . .   **+**

   Add (deduct) changes in Deferred Income Taxes:
   Increase in the account   . . . .   **+**
   Decrease in the account   . . . .   **−**

Net cash provided by operating activities . . . .   **$XXX**

PREPARING A STATEMENT OF CASH FLOWS

There are four basic steps in preparing a statement of cash flows.

1. Find the change that took place in cash flows during the year.

2. Determine the "net cash provided by operating activities" using either the direct or indirect method.

3. Analyze each additional balance sheet account (beyond those analyzed in step 2) and determine whether the change in the account was the result of an investing activity or a financing activity.

4. Categorize the cash flows obtained in steps 2 and 3 into operating, investing, and financing activities. The net result of all of these cash flows should equal the change in cash obtained in step 1.

EXAMPLE OF STATEMENT OF CASH FLOWS

Aspen Company
Comparative Balance Sheets

Assets	19x2	19x1
Current assets:		
Cash	$ 3,000	$ 6,000
Accounts receivable, net	18,000	9,000
Inventory	27,000	15,000
Total current assets	48,000	30,000
Plant and equipment (Note 1)	200,000	189,000
Less accumulated depreciation . . .	98,000	95,000
Net plant and equipment	102,000	94,000
Investments	10,000	6,000
Total assets	$160,000	$130,000

Liabilities & Stockholders' Equity	19x2	19x1
Current liabilities:		
Accounts payable	$ 16,000	$ 10,000
Accrued liabilities	1,000	3,000
Taxes payable	4,000	1,000
Total current liabilities	21,000	14,000
Bonds payable, 10%	36,000	20,000
Stockholders' equity:		
Preferred stock	5,000	12,000
Common stock	38,000	30,000
Retained earnings	60,000	54,000
Total stockholders' equity	103,000	96,000
Total liabilities and equity	$160,000	$130,000

Note 1: Equipment that had cost $7,000 new, and on which there
was accumulated depreciation of $5,000, was sold during the year
for its book value of $2,000.

EXAMPLE OF STATEMENT OF CASH FLOWS
(cont'd)

Aspen Company
Income Statement, 19X2

Sales	$300,000
Less cost of goods sold	100,000
Gross margin	200,000
Less operating expenses (Note 2)	175,000
Net operating income	25,000
Less income taxes	10,000
Net income	$ 15,000

Note 2: The operating expenses include $8,000 in depreciation expense.

Aspen Company
Statement of Retained Earnings, 19X2

Retained earnings, January 1	$ 54,000
Add net income	15,000
Total	69,000
Less dividends:	
Cash dividends, preferred	1,000
Stock dividends, common	8,000
Total dividends	9,000
Retained earnings, December 31	$ 60,000

STEP #1

Aspen Company's cash account decreased by $3,000 during 19x2, as shown on its balance sheet.

STEP #2

Aspen Company's "net cash provided by operating activities" for 19X2 is computed below using the indirect method.

Net income $15,000

Adjustments to convert net income to a cash basis:

Depreciation for the year   8,000

Add (deduct) changes in current asset accounts:
Increase in accounts receivable . . . .   (9,000)
Increase in inventory . . . .   (12,000)

Add (deduct) changes in current liability accounts:
Increase in accounts payable   6,000
Decrease in accrued liabilities . . . .   (2,000)
Increase in taxes payable . . . .   <u>3,000</u>

Net cash provided by operating activities . . . . .   <u>$ 9,000</u>

STEP #3

Each additional account on Aspen Company's balance sheet is analyzed to show the effect of its change on cash during 19x2.

Retained Earnings

Retained Earnings

		54,000	Balance
Cash dividends	1,000	15,000	Net Income
Stock dividends	8,000		
		60,000	Balance

- The $15,000 net income figure has already been included in net cash provided by operating activities.
- The $1,000 in cash dividends is classified as a financing use of cash.
- The $8,000 in stock dividends does not involve a cash flow and does not change total owners' equity; it is simply a change in the composition of owners' equity. (Retained earnings is reduced and common stock is increased.)

Common Stock

The $8,000 increase in the Common Stock account is ignored since it is a consequence of the stock dividend which does not affect total owners' equity.

Preferred Stock

The $7,000 decrease in the Preferred Stock account is classified as a use of cash for financing activities.

Investments

The $4,000 increase in the Investments account is classified as a use of cash for investing activities.

STEP #3 (cont'd)

Bonds Payable

The $16,000 increase in Bonds Payable is classified as cash provided by financing activities.

Plant and Equipment

	Plant and Equipment		
Balance	189,000		
Purchase	?	7,000	Sale
Balance	200,000		

• The $2,000 received on sale of the old equipment (the $7,000 above represents the original cost of the old equipment) is classified as cash provided by investing activities.
• The company must have purchased $18,000 in plant and equipment during the year, which is classified as a use of cash for investing activities.

Accumulated Depreciation

	Accumulated Depreciation		
Depreciation on old equip. 5,000		95,000	Balance
		8,000	Depreciation
		98,000	Balance

• The $8,000 in current depreciation has already been entered as an adjustment in computing the net cash provided by operating activities.

STEP #4

ASPEN COMPANY
Statement of Cash Flows
For the Year Ended December 31, 19x2

Operating Activities

Net cash provided by operating activities* . $ 9,000

Investing activities

Cash was provided by:

    Sale of plant and equipment . . . . . . $ 2,000

Cash was used to:

    Purchase plant and equipment . . . . .   (18,000)

    Purchase investments . . . .   (4,000)

Net cash used for investing activities . . . .   (20,000)

Financing activities

Cash was provided by:

    Issue of bonds   16,000

Cash was used to:

    Retire preferred stock . . . .   (7,000)

    Pay cash dividends to owners . . . . . .   (1,000)

Net cash provided by financing activities . .   8,000

Net decrease in cash and cash equivalents .   (3,000)

Cash and cash equivalents, January 1 . . .   6,000

Cash and cash equivalents, December 31   . $ 3,000

* Due to lack of space, operating activities are not listed here. See Step #2 for the missing details.

WORKING PAPER METHOD

Cash

Provided	Used

Accounts Receivable

Bal.	9,000	
Bal.	18,000	

Inventory

Bal.	15,000	
Bal.	27,000	

Plant and Equipment

Bal.	189,000	
Bal.	200,000	

Accumulated Deprec.

	Bal.	95,000
	Bal.	98,000

Investments

Bal.	6,000	
Bal.	10,000	

Accounts Payable

	Bal.	10,000
	Bal.	16,000

Accrued Liabilities

	Bal.	3,000
	Bal.	1,000

Taxes Payable

	Bal.	1,000
	Bal.	4,000

Bonds Payable

	Bal.	20,000
	Bal.	36,000

Preferred Stock

	Bal.	12,000
	Bal.	5,000

Common Stock

	Bal.	30,000
	Bal.	38,000

Retained Earnings

	Bal.	54,000
	Bal.	60,000

WORKING PAPER METHOD (cont'd)

Accounts Receivable	
Bal. 9,000	
(4) 9,000	
Bal. 18,000	

Inventory	
Bal. 15,000	
(5) 12,000	
Bal. 27,000	

Plant and Equipment	
Bal. 189,000	
(10) 18,000	(11) 7,000
Bal. 200,000	

Accumulated Deprec.	
	Bal. 95,000
(11) 5,000	(6) 8,000
	Bal. 98,000

Investments	
Bal. 6,000	
(12) 4,000	
Bal. 10,000	

Accounts Payable	
	Bal. 10,000
	(7) 6,000
	Bal. 16,000

Accrued Liabilities	
	Bal. 3,000
(8) 2,000	
	Bal. 1,000

Taxes Payable	
	Bal. 1,000
	(9) 3,000
	Bal. 4,000

Bonds Payable	
	Bal. 20,000
	(13) 16,000
	Bal. 36,000

Preferred Stock	
	Bal. 12,000
(14) 7,000	
	Bal. 5,000

Common Stock	
	Bal. 30,000
	(3) 8,000
	Bal. 38,000

Retained Earnings	
	Bal. 54,000
(2) 1,000	(1) 15,000
(3) 8,000	
	Bal. 60,000

WORKING PAPER METHOD (cont'd)

	Cash			
	Provided		Used	
Net income	(1) 15,000		(4) 9,000	Increase in accounts receivable
Increase in accum. deprec.	(6) 8,000		(5) 12,000	Increase in inventory
Increase in accounts payable	(7) 6,000		(8) 2,000	Decrease in accrued liabilities
Increase in taxes payable	(9) 3,000			
Net cash provided by operating activities	9,000			
Sale of plant and equipment	(11) 2,000		(2) 1,000	Payment of cash dividends
Issue of bonds	(13) 16,000		(10) 18,000	Purchase of plant and equipment
			(12) 4,000	Purchase of investments
			(14) 7,000	Retire preferred stock

DIRECT METHOD

Revenue		$300,000
Adjustments to cash basis:		
1. Increase in accounts receivable	−	− 9,000
2. Decrease in accounts receivable	+	_____
Revenue adjusted to cash basis		$291,000
Cost of goods sold		100,000
Adjustments to cash basis:		
3. Increase in inventory	+	+12,000
4. Decrease in inventory	−	
5. Increase in accounts payable	−	− 6,000
6. Decrease in accounts payable	+	_____
Cost of goods sold adjusted to cash basis . .		106,000
Operating expenses		175,000
Adjustments to cash basis:		
7. Increase in accrued liabilities	−	
8. Decrease in accrued liabilities	+	+ 2,000
9. Increase in prepaid expenses	+	
10. Decrease in prepaid expenses	−	
11. Depreciation	−	− 8,000
Operating expenses adjusted to cash basis . .		169,000
Income tax expense		10,000
Adjustments to cash basis:		
12. Increase in accrued taxes payable . . .	−	− 3,000
13. Decreased in accrued taxes payable . .	+	
14. Increase in deferred income taxes . . .	−	
15. Decrease in deferred income taxes . . .	+	_____
Income taxes adjusted to cash basis		7,000
Net cash provided by operating activities		$ 9,000

FINANCIAL STATEMENT ANALYSIS

Few figures appearing on financial statements have much significance by themselves. The relationship of one figure to another and the amount and direction of changes are important.

Several techniques are commonly used to help analyze financial statements. These techniques include:
- Dollar and percentage changes.
- Common-size statements.
- Ratios.

Trend Percentages

Trend percentages state several years' financial data in terms of a base year.

EXAMPLE: Translate the following data into trend percentages.

	19x4	19x3	19x2	19x1
Sales	$650,000	$600,000	$550,000	$500,000
Accounts receivable .	$ 70,000	$ 52,000	$ 44,000	$ 40,000

These data in trend percentage form would be:

	19x4	19x3	19x2	19x1
Sales	130%	120%	110%*	100%
Accounts receivable . .	175%	130%	110%	100%

* $550,000 ÷ $500,000 = 110%, and so forth.

COMPARATIVE STATEMENTS

EXAMPLE: Comparative balance sheets covering the last two years for Molin Company follow (dollar amounts are in thousands).

Comparative Statements of Financial Position

Assets	19x2	19x1	Change Amount	Percent
Current assets:				
Cash	$ 90	$ 300	$ (210)	(70.0)
Accounts receivable . . .	800	500	300	60.0
Inventory	1,400	900	500	55.6
Prepaid expenses	60	60	0	0.0
Total current assets	2,350	1,760	590	33.5
Plant and equipment, net . .	2,650	2,240	410	18.3
Total assets	$5,000	$4,000	$1,000	25.0
Liabilities and Stockholders' Equity				
Liabilities:				
Current liabilities	$1,400	$ 750	$ 650	86.7
Bonds payable, 10%	600	600	0	0.0
Total liabilities	2,000	1,350	650	48.1
Stockholders' equity:				
Preferred stock, $25 par, 7.5%	400	400	0	0.0
Common stock, $10 par . .	500	500	0	0.0
Retained earnings	2,100	1,750	350	20.0
Total stockholders' equity . .	3,000	2,650	350	13.2
Total liabilities and				
stockholders' equity . . .	$5,000	$4,000	$1,000	25.0

COMPARATIVE STATEMENTS (cont'd)

Comparative income statements and retained earnings statements for the last two years for Molin Company follow (dollar amounts are in thousands).

Comparative Income Statements

			Change	
	19x2	19x1	Amount	Percent
Sales	$9,000	$8,000	$1,000	12.5
Cost of goods sold	5,930	5,100	830	16.3
Gross margin	3,070	2,900	170	5.9
Less operating expenses . .	2,160	2,040	120	5.9
Net operating income	910	860	50	5.8
Less interest expense	60	60	0	0.0
Net income before taxes . . .	850	800	50	6.3
Less income taxes (40%) . .	340	320	20	6.3
Net income	$ 510	$ 480	$ 30	6.3

Comparative Retained Earnings Statements

			Change	
	19x2	19x1	Amount	Percent
Retained earnings, beginning	$1,750	$1,420	$330	23.2
Add net income	510	480	30	6.3
Total	2,260	1,900	360	18.9
Deduct dividends paid:				
Preferred stock	30	30	0	0.0
Common stock	130	120	10	8.3
Total	160	150	10	6.7
Retained earnings, end . .	$2,100	$1,750	$350	20.0

COMMON-SIZE STATEMENTS

Common-size balance sheets covering the last two years for the Molin Company follow (dollar amounts are in thousands).

Common-Size Statements of Financial Position

Assets	19x2	19x1	Common-Size Percentages 19x2	19x1
Current assets:				
Cash	$ 90	$ 300	1.8	7.5
Accounts receivable . . .	800	500	16.0	12.5
Inventory	1,400	900	28.0	22.5
Prepaid expenses	60	60	1.2	1.5
Total current assets	2,350	1,760	47.0	44.0
Plant and equipment, net . .	2,650	2,240	53.0	56.0
Total assets	$5,000	$4,000	100.0	100.0
Liabilities and Stockholders' Equity				
Liabilities:				
Current liabilities	$1,400	$ 750	28.0	18.8
Bonds payable, 10%	600	600	12.0	15.0
Total liabilities	2,000	1,350	40.0	33.8
Stockholders' equity:				
Preferred stock, $25 par, 7.5%	400	400	8.0	10.0
Common stock, $10 par . .	500	500	10.0	12.5
Retained earnings	2,100	1,750	42.0	43.7
Total stockholders' equity . .	3,000	2,650	60.0	66.2
Total liabilities and stockholders' equity . . .	$5,000	$4,000	100.0	100.0

COMMON-SIZE STATEMENTS (cont'd)

Common-size income statements covering the last two years
for Molin Company follow (dollar amounts are in thousands).

Common-Size Income Statements

Assets	19x2	19x1	Common-Size Percentages 19x2	19x1
Sales	$9,000	$8,000	100.0	100.0
Cost of goods sold	5,930	5,100	65.9	63.7
Gross margin	3,070	2,900	34.1	36.3
Less operating expenses . .	2,160	2,040	24.0	25.5
Net operating income	910	860	10.1	10.8
Less interest expense	60	60	0.7	0.8
Net income before taxes . . .	850	800	9.4	10.0
Less income taxes (40%) . .	340	320	3.8	4.0
Net income	$ 510	$ 480	5.6	6.0

RATIO ANALYSIS—
THE COMMON STOCKHOLDER

Data for all of the following ratios are taken from the
financial statements of Molin Company on preceding pages.

Earnings Per Share

Earnings per share computations relate only to common stock.
Molin Company's earnings per share would be:

$$\frac{\text{Net income} - \text{Preferred dividends}}{\text{Common shares outstanding}} = \text{Earnings per share}$$

19x2

$$\frac{\$510,000 - \$30,000}{50,000 \text{ shares*}} = \$9.60$$

19x1

$$\frac{\$480,000 - \$30,000}{50,000 \text{ shares}} = \$9.00$$

$$* \ \frac{\$500,000 \text{ common stock}}{\$10 \text{ par value per share of common stock}} = 50,000 \text{ shares}$$

Fully Diluted EPS

Assume that each of Molin Company's 16,000 shares of
preferred stock ($400,000 ÷ $25 par = 16,000 shares) is convertible
into three shares of common stock.

$$\frac{\text{Net income}}{\text{Original shares} + \text{Converted shares}} = \text{Fully diluted EPS}$$

19x2

$$\frac{\$510,000}{50,000 + 48,000 \text{ shares}} = \$5.20$$

19x1

$$\frac{\$480,000}{50,000 + 48,000 \text{ shares}} = \$4.90$$

Price—Earnings Ratio

The relationship between the market price of a share of stock and the stock's current earnings per share is often stated in terms of a price-earnings ratio. Assume that Molin Company's stock is now selling for $72 per share and that last year it sold for $63 per share.

$$\frac{\text{Market price per share}}{\text{Earnings per share}} = \text{Price—earnings ratio}$$

19x2

$$\frac{\$72}{\$9.60} = 7.5 \text{ times}$$

19x1

$$\frac{\$63}{\$9.00} = 7.0 \text{ times}$$

Dividend Payout Ratio

The dividend payout ratio gauges the portion of current earnings being paid out as dividends to common stockholders. The dividend in 19x2 was $2.60 per share ($130,000 ÷ 50,000 shares), and in 19x1 it was $2.40 per share ($120,000 ÷ 50,000 shares).

$$\frac{\text{Dividends per share}}{\text{Earnings per share}} = \text{Dividend payout ratio}$$

19x2

$$\frac{\$2.60}{\$9.60} = 27.1\%$$

19x1

$$\frac{\$2.40}{\$9.00} = 26.7\%$$

The amount of dividends paid out differs by industry; there is no "right" payout ratio.

Dividend Yield Ratio

The dividend yield ratio measures the cash return being provided by a stock.

$$\frac{\text{Dividends per share}}{\text{Market price per share}} = \text{Dividend yield ratio}$$

$$\underline{\quad 19x2 \quad}$$
$$\frac{\$2.60}{\$72} = 3.6\%$$

$$\underline{\quad 19x1 \quad}$$
$$\frac{\$2.40}{\$63} = 3.8\%$$

A low dividend payout ratio and a low dividend yield ratio indicate that the company is retaining its earnings for internal reinvestment.

Return On Total Assets

The return on total assets ratio is a measure of how well assets have been employed by management. Assume that total assets in Molin Company were $3,200,000 at the beginning of 19x1.

$$\frac{\text{Net income} + [\text{Interest expense} \times (1 - \text{Tax rate})]}{\text{Average total assets}} = \frac{\text{Return on}}{\text{total assets}}$$

$$\underline{\quad 19x2 \quad}$$
$$\frac{\$510{,}000 + (\$60{,}000 \times 0.60)}{(\$5{,}000{,}000 + \$4{,}000{,}000)/2} = 12.1\%$$

$$\underline{\quad 19x1 \quad}$$
$$\frac{\$480{,}000 + (\$60{,}000 \times 0.60)}{(\$4{,}000{,}000 + \$3{,}200{,}000)/2} = 14.3\%$$

By adding interest expense back to net income, the return on assets is not influenced by the way in which the assets were financed.

Return On Common Stockholders' Equity

Common stockholders' equity consists of total stockholders' equity less preferred stock. Common stockholders' equity in Molin Company was $1,920,000 at the beginning of 19x1.

$$\frac{\text{Net income} - \text{Preferred dividends}}{\text{Average common stockholders' equity}} = \frac{\text{Return on common}}{\text{stockholders' equity}}$$

19x2

$$\frac{\$510,000 - \$30,000}{(\$2,600,000 + \$2,250,000)/2} = 19.8\%$$

19x1

$$\frac{\$480,000 - \$30,000}{(\$2,250,000 + \$1,920,000)/2} = 21.6\%$$

Since the return on common stockholders' equity is greater than the return on total assets, financial leverage is positive in both years.

Book Value Per Share

Book value per share shows the amount of common stockholders' equity per share of common stock.

$$\frac{\text{Common stockholders' equity}}{\text{Number of common shares}} = \frac{\text{Book value}}{\text{per share}}$$

19x2

$$\frac{\$2,600,000}{50,000 \text{ shares}} = \$52$$

19x1

$$\frac{\$2,250,000}{50,000 \text{ shares}} = \$45$$

RATIO ANALYSIS—
THE SHORT-TERM CREDITOR

Working Capital

The excess of current assets over current liabilities is known as working capital. Molin Company's working capital is:

	19x2	19x1
Current assets	$2,350,000	$1,760,000
Current liabilities	1,400,000	750,000
Working capital	$ 950,000	$1,010,000

Working capital represents current assets financed from long-term capital sources. Thus, it is viewed as a cushion of protection for short-term creditors.

Current Ratio

The relationship between current assets and current liabilities can also be expressed in terms of the current ratio:

$$\frac{\text{Current assets}}{\text{Current liabilities}} = \text{Current ratio}$$

19x2	19x1
$\dfrac{\$2,350,000}{\$1,400,000} = 1.68 \text{ to } 1$	$\dfrac{\$1,760,000}{\$750,000} = 2.35 \text{ to } 1$

A declining current ratio may be a sign of a deteriorating financial condition.

Acid-Test Ratio

The acid-test ratio (or quick ratio) provides a more rigorous test than the current ratio of a company's ability to settle its short-term liabilities.

$$\frac{\text{Cash + Marketable securities + Current receivables}}{\text{Current liabilities}} = \text{Acid–test ratio}$$

19x2

$$\frac{\$90,000 + \$800,000}{\$1,400,000} = 0.64 \text{ to } 1$$

19x1

$$\frac{\$300,000 + \$500,000}{\$750,000} = 1.07 \text{ to } 1$$

Accounts Receivable Turnover

The accounts receivable turnover indicates how quickly accounts receivables are collected. Assume that the accounts receivable balance for Molin Company was $300,000 at the beginning of 19x1.

$$\frac{\text{Sales on account}}{\text{Average accounts receivable balance}} = \text{Accounts receivable turnover}$$

$$\frac{\text{365 days}}{\text{Accounts receivable turnover}} = \text{Average collection period}$$

19x2

$$\frac{\$9,000,000}{(\$800,000 + \$500,000)/2} = 13.8 \text{ times}$$

19x1

$$\frac{\$8,000,000}{(\$500,000 + \$300,000)/2} = 20.0 \text{ times}$$

$$\frac{\text{365 days}}{13.8 \text{ times}} = 26.4 \text{ days}$$

$$\frac{\text{365 days}}{20.0 \text{ times}} = 18.3 \text{ days}$$

Inventory Turnover

The inventory turnover ratio measures how quickly inventory is converted into sales. Assume that Molin Company's inventory balance was $700,000 at the beginning of 19x1.

$$\frac{\text{Cost of goods sold}}{\text{Average inventory balance}} = \text{Inventory turnover}$$

$$\frac{365 \text{ days}}{\text{Inventory turnover}} = \frac{\text{Average days}}{\text{to sell inventory}}$$

19x2	19x1
$\dfrac{\$5,930,000}{(\$1,400,000+\$900,000)/2}=5.2 \text{ times}$	$\dfrac{\$5,100,000}{(\$900,000+\$700,000)/2}=6.4 \text{ times}$
$\dfrac{365 \text{ days}}{5.2 \text{ times}} = 70.2 \text{ days}$	$\dfrac{365 \text{ days}}{6.4 \text{ times}} = 57.0 \text{ days}$

RATIO ANALYSIS—
THE LONG-TERM CREDITOR

Times Interest Earned

The times interest earned ratio is widely used as a measure of the ability of a firm's operations to provide protection for long-term creditors.

$$\frac{\text{Earnings before interest and taxes}}{\text{Interest expense}} = \text{Times interest earned}$$

19x2

$$\frac{\$910}{\$60} = 15.2 \text{ times}$$

19x1

$$\frac{\$860}{\$60} = 14.3 \text{ times}$$

Debt-To-Equity Ratio

The debt-to-equity ratio measures the amount of assets being provided by creditors for each dollar of assets being provided by owners.

$$\frac{\text{Total liabilities}}{\text{Stockholders' equity}} = \text{Debt–to–equity ratio}$$

19x2

$$\frac{\$2,000,000}{\$3,000,000} = 0.67 \text{ to } 1$$

19x1

$$\frac{\$1,350,000}{\$2,650,000} = 0.51 \text{ to } 1$$

There is no "right" amount of debt for a firm to carry. Since different industries face different risks, the level of debt that is appropriate will vary from industry to industry.

QUALITY COSTS

QUALITY OF CONFORMANCE

A product or service can have many attractive features and be well-designed, but it can still be considered low quality if there are defects in the final product. <u>Quality of conformance</u> is the degree to which the actual product meets its design specifications and is free of defects.

COSTS ASSOCIATED WITH DEFECTS

The costs of fixing or scrapping defective units before they reach customers are called <u>internal failure costs</u>.

Costs that are incurred by releasing defective units to customers are called <u>external failure costs</u>. These costs include:
- Costs of fixing defective products under warranty.
- Intangible costs such as loss of sales due to a tarnished reputation.

There are two ways of avoiding the costs of internal and external failures:
- Prevent defects.
- Inspect and test units before they are released.

The costs associated with these activities are called <u>prevention costs</u> and <u>appraisal costs</u>.

EXAMPLES OF QUALITY COSTS

Prevention Costs
Systems development
Quality engineering
Quality training
Quality circles
Statistical process control
Supervision of prevention
Quality data gathering,
    analysis, and reporting
Quality improvement projects
Technical support to suppliers
Audits of effectiveness of
    the quality system

Appraisal Costs
Test and inspection of
    incoming materials
Test and inspection of
    in-process goods
Final product testing and
    inspection
Supplies used in testing
    and inspection
Depreciation of test
    equipment
Maintenance of test
    equipment
Setups for testing
Utilities in the inspection area
Field testing at customer site

Internal Failure Costs
Net cost of scrap
Net cost of spoilage
Rework labor and spoilage
Reinspection of reworked units
Retesting of reworked units
Downtime caused by defects
Disposal of defective units
Analysis of causes of defects
Re-entering data due to
    keypunch errors
Correcting software errors

External Failure Costs
Cost of field servicing, and
    handling complaints
Warranty repairs
Warranty replacements
Repairs and replacements
    beyond warranty period
Product recalls
Liability from defective
    products
Returns and allowances from
    quality problems
Lost sales from a reputation
    for poor quality

TRADING-OFF QUALITY COSTS

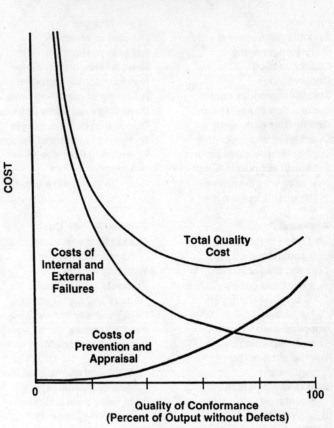

QUALITY COST REPORT
(Exhibit K-4)

VENTURA COMPANY
Quality Cost Report
For Years 1 and 2

	Year 2		Year 1	
	Amount	Percent*	Amount	Percent*
Prevention costs:				
Systems development	$ 400,000	0.80	$ 270,000	0.54
Quality training.	210,000	0.42	130,000	0.26
Supervision of prevention activities	70,000	0.14	40,000	0.08
Quality improvement projects	320,000	0.64	210,000	0.42
Total	1,000,000	2.00	650,000	1.30
Appraisal costs:				
Inspection	600,000	1.20	560,000	1.12
Reliability testing	580,000	1.16	420,000	0.84
Supervision of testing and inspection	120,000	0.24	80,000	0.16
Depreciation of test equipment	200,000	0.40	140,000	0.28
Total	1,500,000	3.00	1,200,000	2.40
Internal failure costs:				
Net cost of scrap	900,000	1.80	750,000	1.50
Rework labor and overhead	1,430,000	2.86	810,000	1.62
Downtime due to defects in quality	170,000	0.34	100,000	0.20
Disposal of defective products	500,000	1.00	340,000	0.68
Total	3,000,000	6.00	2,000,000	4.00
External failure costs:				
Warranty repairs	400,000	0.80	900,000	1.80
Warranty replacements	870,000	1.74	2,300,000	4.60
Allowances	130,000	0.26	630,000	1.26
Cost of field servicing	600,000	1.20	1,320,000	2.64
Total	2,000,000	4.00	5,150,000	10.30
Total quality cost	$7,500,000	15.00	$9,000,000	18.00

* As a percentage of total sales. We assume that in each year sales totaled $50,000,000.

QUALITY COST REPORT IN GRAPHIC FORM
(Exhibit K-5)

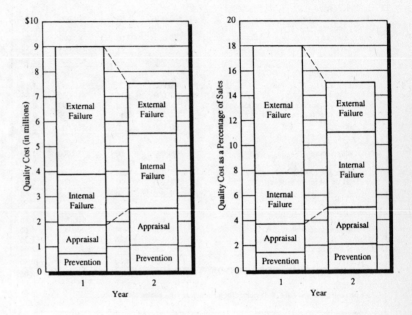

USES OF QUALITY COST REPORTS

Quality cost reports make visible information that is usually buried in general overhead.

- Managers are often surprised by how much defects cost. Prevention and appraisal are expensive, but so too are internal and external failures. The magnitude of the costs often energizes managers to take action.

- Quality cost information helps identify where the biggest quality problems lie. For example, if scrap is a big cost, efforts should be devoted to reducing scrap through prevention.

- Quality cost information helps assess how resources should be distributed. If internal and external failure costs are high relative to prevention and appraisal costs, more should probably be spent on prevention and appraisal.

- Quality cost reports can be used as a basis for budgeting quality improvement programs.

Since quality cost reports are largely an attention-directing device, the costs do not have to be precise. Unfortunately, one very important cost is usually excluded from the reports due to measurement difficulties — the cost of lost sales due to external failures.

PRICING DECISIONS

BACKGROUND

Clearly, the price of a product or service should exceed its out-of-pocket costs. Unfortunately, it is difficult to know by how much the price should exceed those costs.

- The dilemma is that price and unit sales move in opposite directions—the higher the price, the lower unit sales.

- In most situations, pricing should largely be a marketing decision that takes into account this delicate balance between price and unit sales.

Nevertheless, some type of cost-plus pricing formula is commonly used as a starting point in the pricing decision.

COST-PLUS PRICING FORMULAS

Under cost-plus pricing, the target selling price is computed by applying a predetermined markup to a cost base. Two cost bases are commonly used—absorption costs or variable costs. When absorption costs are used as the cost base in cost-plus pricing, it is called the absorption approach. When variable costs are used, it is called the contribution approach and the variable costs include all variable costs—not just manufacturing.

THE ABSORPTION APPROACH

Under the absorption approach to cost-plus pricing:

- **The cost base consists of the fixed and variable manufacturing costs required to make a unit.**

- **The markup must be high enough to cover selling and administrative expenses and to provide for a profit.**

EXAMPLE: Aspen Company hopes to sell 20,000 units next year. Cost data concerning this product follow:

Direct materials	$6 per unit
Direct labor	$4 per unit
Variable manufacturing overhead	$1 per unit
Fixed manufacturing overhead	$380,000 per year
Variable selling & admin. expense	$4 per unit
Fixed selling & admin. expense	$100,000 per year

Assume that target selling prices are determined by adding a 40% markup to the cost to manufacture a unit.

Direct materials	$ 6
Direct labor	4
Variable manufacturing overhead	1
Fixed manufacturing overhead ($380,000 ÷ 20,000) . .	19
Total cost to manufacture a unit	30
Markup at 40% of cost to manufacture	12
Target selling price	$42

THE MARKUP ON AN ABSORPTION BASIS

The 40% markup on unit manufacturing costs could be:
- an industry practice.
- a time-honored thumbrule in the company.
- managers' judgment of how much markup the market will bear.
- the result of a markup computation.

MARKUP COMPUTATION

The markup on absorption costs, *given the assumed unit sales volume*, can be determined from the following formula.

$$\text{Markup percentage on absorption cost} = \frac{\text{Desired return on assets employed} + \text{Selling and admin. expenses}}{\text{Volume in units X Unit cost to manufacture}}$$

EXAMPLE: Suppose Aspen Company desires a 15% return on assets (ROI) and has $400,000 in assets.

Desired return on assets employed = .15 X $400,0000 = $60,000
Volume in units = 20,000 units
Selling and admin. expenses = $4 X 20,000 + $100,000 = $180,000
Unit cost to manufacture = $30 (see previous calculations)

$$\frac{\$60,000 + \$180,000}{20,000 \text{ units X } \$30 \text{ per unit}} = \frac{\$240,000}{\$600,000} = 40\%$$

VERIFICATION OF THE MARKUP

• Suppose 20,000 units are sold as planned at the price of $42
per unit. The net income of Aspen Company would be $60,000,
which is the desired return on assets employed:

Income Statement
Aspen Company
20,000 units

Revenue ($42 X 20,000)	$840,000
COGS ($30 X 20,000)	600,000
Gross margin	240,000
Selling and admin.	
expenses ($4 X 20,000 + $100,000)	180,000
Net income	$ 60,000

WEAKNESSES OF THE ABSORPTION APPROACH

• In order to arrive at the selling price, some sales volume must be assumed under the absorption approach. However, in reality the sales volume depends upon the selling price.

• If the sales volume turns out to the be less than assumed, there will be less profit than desired and possibly a loss. The protection provided by the markup is more illusory than real.

• As unit sales volume drops, the unit production cost increases as fixed production costs are spread across fewer units. Applying a preset markup to this higher unit production cost results in higher selling prices. This further depresses unit sales volume, which leads to an increase in selling prices, and so on. A temporary decline in unit sales due to a recession could lead to disastrous over-reaction if cost-plus pricing is followed too rigidly.

THE CONTRIBUTION APPROACH

Under the contribution approach to cost-plus pricing:

- **The cost base consists of all of the variable costs associated with the product — both manufacturing and nonmanufacturing.**

- **The markup must be high enough to cover both fixed costs and the desired profit.**

EXAMPLE: We will use the Aspen Company again to illustrate the contribution approach to cost-plus pricing.

Direct materials	$6 per unit
Direct labor	$4 per unit
Variable manufacturing overhead	$1 per unit
Fixed manufacturing overhead	$380,000 per year
Variable selling & admin. expense	$4 per unit
Fixed selling & admin. expense	$100,000 per year

Assume that target selling prices are determined by adding a 180% markup to unit variable cost.

Direct materials	$ 6
Direct labor	4
Variable manufacturing overhead	1
Variable selling & admin. expense	4
Unit variable cost	15
Markup at 180% of unit variable costs	27
Target selling price	$42

THE MARKUP ON AN CONTRIBUTION BASIS

As with the absorption cost approach, the 180% markup on variable costs could be:
- an industry practice.
- a time-honored thumbrule in the company.
- managers' judgment of how much markup the market will bear.
- the result of a markup computation.

MARKUP COMPUTATION

The markup on variable cost, *given the assumed unit sales volume*, can be determined from the following formula.

$$\text{Markup percentage on variable cost} = \frac{\text{Desired return on assets employed} + \text{Fixed costs}}{\text{Volume in units} \times \text{Unit variable costs}}$$

EXAMPLE: Suppose Aspen Company desires a 15% return on assets (ROI), has $400,000 in assets, and anticipates a volume of 20,000 units.

Desired return on assets employed = .15 X $400,000 = $60,000
Fixed costs = $380,000 + $100,000 = $480,000
Volume in units = 20,000 units
Unit variable cost = $15

$$\frac{\$60,000 + \$480,000}{20,000 \text{ units} \times \$15 \text{ per unit}} = \frac{\$540,000}{\$300,000} = 180\%$$

OBSERVATIONS CONCERNING
COST-PLUS PRICING

- Even though the term "cost-plus" is used to describe these methods, part of the costs are buried in the plus, or markup, portion of the formula under both the absorption costing and contribution approaches.

- Economists argue that the contribution approach should be used, but the markup applied to variable costs should depend upon how sensitive customers are to price.

  - If the consumers of a particular product will cut their purchases dramatically because of a small increase in price, then the markup on that product should be small.

  - If consumers of a particular product are not particularly sensitive to price, then the markup on that product should be relatively large.

- While target prices set with formulas can be helpful as a starting point, the final pricing decision should involve marketing judgment as well as cost considerations.

TARGET COSTING

A number of firms, particularly in Japan, approach the pricing problem from an entirely different perspective.

TRADITIONAL APPROACH

The cost-plus pricing approach takes cost as given and marks it up. Unfortunately, the cost of a product may be so high using this approach that the company may price itself out of the market.

TARGET COSTING APPROACH

Companies that use the target costing approach turn the traditional approach on its head. These companies believe that the market, not the company, ultimately determines prices.

In the target costing approach, the selling price is taken as a given and the company strives to design and manufacture the product so that its cost is low enough to yield a satisfactory profit.

Target costing is a market-driven approach that puts the emphasis on managing how things are done inside the company, rather than hoping that consumers will accept a price high enough to cover all of the costs the company has incurred.

TIME AND MATERIAL PRICING

Service organizations (repair shops, printing shops, attorneys, etc.) often use a pricing method called time and material pricing.

Under this method, two pricing rates are established—one based on labor time and the other based on materials used.

EXAMPLE: Speedy Appliance Repair incurs the following costs in a typical year:

	Service	*Parts*
Service employee wages	$260,000	
Parts employee wages		$ 40,000
Shop supervision	36,000	
Parts supervision		38,000
Fringe benefits	59,000	15,000
Supplies	6,000	2,000
Utilities	12,000	5,000
Rent	30,000	15,000
Depreciation	40,000	5,000
Other	7,000	2,000
Total	$450,000	$122,000

The costs of parts used in repairs are billed directly to customers and are not included in the above table.

Time Component

The service personnel work a total of 15,000 billable hours in a typical year. Based on this data and a desired margin of $5 per billable hour, the labor time rate would be determined as follows:

Service costs per billable hour ($450,000 ÷ 15,000) . . . $30
Desired margin per billable hour . . . . ____5
Time component charge $35

Thus, customers will be charged $35 per hour for service personnel time.

Material Component

The $122,000 cost of the parts department is recovered by marking up the invoice cost of parts ($305,000 per year). In addition, the company adds a 20% profit margin to the invoice cost.

Charge for ordering, handling, and
   carrying parts ($122,000÷$305,000)   40% of invoice cost
Desired profit margin on parts   20% of invoice cost
Material loading charge   60% of invoice cost

Thus, the amount charged for parts on a job will consist of the invoice cost of the parts plus a material loading charge equal to 60% of this cost.

BILLING A JOB

In billing a job, the time and material components are added together to get the total price to be charged.

Example: To complete the Speedy Appliance Repair example, assume that a repair job is completed that required 3 hours of labor time and $40 in parts.

Time charge: (3 hours X $35)		$105
Materials charge:		
Invoice cost of parts	$40	
Material loading charge ($40 X 60%)	24	64
Total price of the job		$169

Notes

Notes

Notes